Master Your Taxes
How to maximize
your after-tax returns

Evelyn Jacks

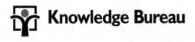 **Knowledge Bureau**

WINNIPEG, MANITOBA, CANADA

Evelyn Jacks

MASTER YOUR TAXES
How to maximize your after-tax returns

©2008 Knowledge Bureau, Inc.

ISBN No. 978-1-897526-07-1

Printed and bound in Canada

Canadian Cataloguing in Publication Data

Jacks, Evelyn, 1955-
    Master your taxes: how to maximize your after-tax returns / Evelyn Jacks.

Includes Index

1. Income tax – Canada – Popular works. 2. Income tax deductions – Canada – Popular works. 3. Tax planning – Canada – Popular works. I. Title.

HJ4661.J213 2008   343.7105'2   C2008-907905-1

Publisher:
Knowledge Bureau, Inc.
Box 52042 Niakwa Postal Outlet, Winnipeg, Manitoba Canada R2M 0Z0
204-953-4769 Email: reception@knowledgebureau.com

Research Assistance: Walter Harder and Associates
Editorial Assistance: Tamara Baker
Cover and Page Design: Sharon Jones

Acknowledgements

Family. Love. Friendship. Time. Health. I am truly blessed and grateful.

Special thanks to my colleagues and associates at The Knowledge Bureau, Sharon, Tamara, Walter.

Al, Cordell and Don for your love and support.

Knowledge Bureau
CANADA'S LEADING EDUCATOR IN TAX AND FINANCIAL SERVICES

Presents
Financial Education for Decision Makers

The Master Your Personal Finances Books:

Master Your Taxes
How to maximize your after-tax returns

Master Your Retirement
How to fulfill your dreams with peace of mind

Master Your Investment in the Family Business
How to increase after-tax wealth

Master Your Money Management
How to manage the advisors who work for you

Master Your Real Wealth
How to live your life with financial security

FREE UPDATING SERVICES

Keep up your Mastery! For the latest in tax and personal financial planning strategies subscribe to Breaking Tax and Investment News. Visit www.knowledgebureau.com/masteryourtaxes

Knowledge Bureau

Contents

Introduction

It's difficult to be an expert at something you do only once a year...
yet expertise is exactly what is required to manage the biggest eroder of
your wealth: the federal and provincial taxes you will pay throughout
your lifetime on your income and capital.

This book will help you soothe that pain by showing you how to master
and control the size of your largest lifetime expense—your taxes—with
a simpler approach to saving time and money.

You will be able to better understand tax lingo, and cut through the
annual process of tax filing to move to the next step: more effective
financial decisions about your income and capital so you can build and
preserve more wealth, though every economic and personal life cycle,
using the tax system as your ally.

You will learn, at a high level, how to get the best after-tax returns from
your income and your investments looking specifically at tax-efficient
decision making for:

- Family Filing
- Occupation and Career
- Financing and Investments
- Future Planning and Family Legacy

We have focused on providing you with need-to-know information, to master your relationships with both the Canada Revenue Agency (CRA) and your team of financial advisors who will help you build wealth throughout your life. Learn how to:

- Understand important tax milestones at each stage of your life
- Take control of the first dollar you earn
- Grasp the real impact of taxes on your income and capital
- Avoid trouble with the taxman and know your rights
- Ask the right probing questions of your advisors
- Make tax-wise decisions about your career options
- Make more as a family unit by splitting income with family members
- Learn the basic principles of tax-free and tax-efficient investing
- Plan for life events like personal residence purchases and family education
- Structure your retirement—legally—to beat the taxman
- Plan a tax-efficient future and peace of mind
- Master the Tax Facts—by cutting through the details to make new tax provisions work for you

With the right people and plans you can build the strategy and processes to Master Your Taxes. These principles will prepare you to make better decisions on your strategic journey to financial freedom, paved with the hundreds of thousands of dollars in tax savings you deserve.

It is, after all, your legal right and duty to arrange your affairs within the framework of the law to pay the least amount of taxes possible. If you are or want to become a prudent steward of your family's financial resources, you will want to know how to accumulate, grow, preserve, and transition your real wealth.

THE FORMAT OF THIS BOOK

The principles for Mastering Your Taxes are discussed in this book in a straight forward fashion, with common features to empower you. In each chapter you will find:

- *A True to Life Scenario:* These feature fictitious families in real-life situations are a backdrop for the principles discussed in the chapter.
- *The Issues:* What is important and why?
- *The Solutions:* What do you need to know to make the right financial decisions for your time and money? How can you best integrate these solutions in your strategic plan to meet goals by asking the right questions?
- *The Mastery:* Tips and Traps to help put your financial decision making into focus, simplify your efforts, and get better results.

We hope you will find this format fruitful in taking control and making better financial decisions—after tax—either on your own, or together with your team of financial advisors.

EVELYN JACKS AND
THE KNOWLEDGE BUREAU

CHAPTER 1

Master The Big Picture

A hero is someone who understands the responsibility that comes with his freedom. BOB DYLAN

Every year Julia dreaded the annual tax filing deadline. She shuddered at the amount of time it would take to gather the myriad of receipts and logs she was supposed to have kept all year long to maximize the multitude of tax deductions and credits, the details of which she was simply not remembering from one year to the next.

"I'm intelligent, I supervise many people at work, and I do a good job keeping the department on budget. Why can't I master my family's tax returns?" she asked a colleague at work, after yet another expensive and frustrating stint with her tax accountant. "It doesn't seem to matter how much I pay in professional fees, I always walk away from the experience feeling that I have paid too much tax and that someone else in my situation is probably taking home more money, after tax. Worse, when it comes to having money left over for my savings, there just isn't much left."

"I don't even know what questions I should be asking," replied her colleague. "Yet I know I am poorer, because of it. What a frustrating waste of time and money!"

THE ISSUES

Many people are acutely aware that getting a handle on their taxes is important. Yet figuring out the "big picture" feels difficult for most. The job seems so big and detail-oriented that you just can't muster the energy to get started, despite the fact that managing those details *will help you become richer!*

By mastering your taxes and taking advantage of all the provisions you are entitled to under law, you will pay less tax, and make and save more money, allowing you to build more real wealth over your lifetime. In short, you will take control of more of the money you make.

The issue and your key to success in financial decision making is this: how can you plan to put and keep more money in your own pocket for as long as possible when the taxman seems to take so much of it first? There is much you can do to ensure you pay the correct amount of tax and not one cent more. The benefits are exponential: you will be poised to make better financial decisions because *you get to work with more money, first.*

When you work to accomplish this, you will accumulate more wealth, faster, giving you more choice and peace of mind. If you are serious about taking control of your money, mastering your taxes is not only important, but absolutely necessary. It will be your largest lifetime expense. In short, you need to position yourself to work with larger, pre-tax dollars, *sooner.*

THE SOLUTIONS

Mastering your taxes is really about overcoming two pain points: time and money. No one has a lot of time, yet that is exactly what it appears to take to figure it out or understand taxes. Worse yet, it seems to require expensive professional advice to get it right.

Here's the good news: you need to make only three simple, strategic decisions to get a handle on your time and after tax results:

- **Earn, tax efficiently.** You are probably quite good at how you earn your living. It's important to keep your revenue flowing. Your new goal is to discover what you can do to accumulate and preserve wealth without "tax leakage."
- **Pay enough, but no more.** To take control and exercise your legal right to pay only the correct amount of tax, not a cent more, you need to shift your focus from annual tax preparation to a strategic plan for tax-efficiency all year round.
- **Get organized and get help.** Most people relate the word "tax" with "tax return preparation," thereby losing focus on the real win: tax planning for your future. To master the annual tax filing pain point, get organized and get professional help. Most of us wouldn't fix our own cars, fly our own planes or perform brain surgery on our family members. Why wouldn't you seek the best help there is for something as potentially lucrative as reconciling your after-tax position for a whole year's work? However, you do need to commit to understanding some basics about your tax return to maximize your relationship with your tax professional.

EARN, TAX EFFICIENTLY

Tax-efficiency is the skill of managing the money you make, so as to receive more of it first, then avoiding or deferring taxes payable for as long as possible, ultimately to pay the least possible as a family unit. When your earnings are tax-efficient you'll build more *real* wealth: what's left after tax, inflation, and your costs.

It's important that you focus on your skills to keep earning and saving top dollars first. However, you should also know that to diversify away tax risk, a variety of income sources may bring better after-tax results. We'll discuss this in later chapters, so you can better discuss it with your advisors.

There are a couple of tools we use to help you understand your "big picture" when it comes to tax.

Marginal Tax Rates

A taxpayer's MTR (Marginal Tax Rate) is a useful tool in measuring tax-efficiency of income sources. It will tell you how much tax you'll pay on the next dollar you plan to earn, while measuring the effect of that income on your eligibility for tax credits and social benefits delivered through the tax system. To compute it, you need to understand that your income sources will be classified into several broad categories for tax purposes. For example:

1. **Ordinary income:** is fully taxable and includes income from employment, pensions, and interest.
2. **Income from self-employment:** is reported on a net basis— what's left after revenues are reduced by allowable deductions.
3. **Capital gains:** are reported upon the disposition (sale or transfer) of an asset. Only half those gains, net of losses, are reported on the return. Sometimes, gains can be avoided when certain properties are donated to charity.
4. **Dividends** are the after-tax distribution of profits from private or public corporations to shareholders. Reporting them involves an integration of the corporate and personal tax systems, the end result of which is a preferential tax rate.

These income sources may also vary by province. A sample of the marginal tax rates levied by various provinces on these various income sources is included in the final chapter of this book for your information. Updates are posted regularly at www.knowledgebureau.com.

It's important to keep on top of these marginal tax rates so you can easily see the advantages of earning a variety of different income sources which will strategically *average down the taxes you pay*.

A quick way to determine the MTR for ordinary income is to add the federal tax rate and the provincial tax rate for your current tax bracket. However, this method does not take into account "clawback zones", or things like provincial surtaxes.

- **A clawback** refers to a reduction of a refundable or non-refundable tax credit or other social benefit because the taxpayer's income has risen above a certain income level. This is essentially a tax on the middle class.
- **A surtax** is a tax on a tax. This will sometimes apply when income has risen to a certain level...it's a tax on the wealthy.

It is therefore more insightful to understand your MTR as it relates to both your tax bracket and the clawback of benefits, surtaxes, and provincial variations you are subject to. This generally requires the help of tax software or a tax accountant who can prepare the calculations for you.

The MTR is therefore an effective tool in determining whether it's worthwhile for you to earn more of the same type of income or consider increasing your wealth—and your eligibility for tax benefits—with different tax-preferred investments, like a contribution to an RRSP (Registered Retirement Savings Plan).

RRSPs, for example, will reduce your Net Income, the figure used to determine the size of clawbacks to tax credits and social benefits. Understanding the impact of a contribution to an RRSP on your tax filing results will allow you to do some tax planning to build real wealth. To show you how effective this can be, consider Lance, an Ontario father whose MTR is 44%:

> By contributing $100 to his RRSP Lance's tax practitioner computes a tax benefit of $44. His refund would increase by $40 and in addition, his family's Child Tax Benefit would increase by $4.
>
> In other words, Lance gets a 44% return on every dollar invested in his RRSP by way of reduced taxes and increased benefits—that's before taking into account the tax-sheltered compounding of investment earnings within the RRSP. That's a great return on your investment, by any standards.

So the big picture is this: know your marginal tax rate on the next dollars you earn so you can make choices about your income sources and tax-preferred investments to get the after tax results you want.

Effective Tax Rates

Do you know how much tax you actually paid last year? What percentage of your total income did you give up? If you don't know, dig out your tax return and look at Line 435 (Taxes Payable) and calculate your effective rate of tax on your total income. Divide Taxes Payable (line 435) by Total Income (line 150). That gives you your actual rate of tax on total income.

That's what ultimately counts—the money that left your pocket. Will your effective tax rate increase or decrease this year? What can you do to reduce the actual taxes you pay on your total taxable income? Are you claiming all the deductions and credits you are entitled to? You need to understand the basic components of the tax return to ask better questions and take control of actual tax outcomes.

PAY ENOUGH BUT NO MORE

People are afraid of the taxman—non-compliance after all comes with heavy fines and potentially jail for tax evaders! But what about addressing the fear of not getting the refund you were hoping for, or the fear that you have missed filing for deductions and credits worth thousands of dollars to your family?

A well managed action plan will help you get over your tax fears. You want to make it your mission to pay only the correct amount of tax and no more. And that's your legal right and duty.

It's important to avoid trouble with the taxman, as we will explain in more detail later, because non-compliance can be very expensive and can seriously erode your carefully managed wealth. Once you better understand the scope of your relationship with CRA, you can masterfully proceed to implement your rights to keep more of your real wealth, which will be the focus of the rest of this book.

Remember, *real wealth management* is the accumulation, growth, preservation, and transition of your personal net worth—after tax, costs, and inflation.[1] It's the number we keep an eye on when we actually have

---

[1] Real Wealth Management is a trademark of The Knowledge Bureau.

to cash in and use our financial resources to fund needs and wants. When you manage the largest eroder of wealth—your personal taxes— you'll be positioned to increase your purchasing power.

GET ORGANIZED AND GET HELP

To build real wealth—that is, what's left for your use, after-tax—the first obstacle to master is your relationship with the CRA. Here's what you need to know.

Canada Revenue Agency (CRA) does so much more than just collect taxes on behalf of the Department of Finance. Our tax system also delivers social and economic policy goals. For many, filing a tax return is the application form for a variety of benefits from government, which taxfilers are happy to receive, and the gateway to tax-preferred investment savings, as illustrated below:

- **To receive tax refunds:** Employees must file a tax return to recover overpaid taxes resulting from overly generous source remittances, demanded from employers by governments. Others may have overpaid quarterly instalment payments or qualified for deductions and credits at year end, all of which can provide for the tax refund.
- **Eligibility for Old Age Security**.
- **Eligibility for refundable tax credits:** like the monthly Child Tax Benefit.
- **Eligibility to make tax-preferred investments:** like the new Tax-Free Savings Account (TFSA) or Registered Retirement Savings Account (RRSP), for which investors must file a tax return to qualify for investment "room".
- **Eligibility for the Canada Pension Plan:** The government counts on entrepreneurs to self-assess and report income, deductions, and taxes owing. It is from these figures that the proprietor's Canada Pension Plan funding is determined and remitted.

There are other dynamics which affect tax compliance negatively, as they cause average people—no matter how astute and committed they are to the principle of tax fairness—to avoid, ignore, or file their taxes incorrectly to their ultimate disadvantage:

- Often money is owed to government, but can't be paid.
- Tax law is too complex, changes too quickly, and is not well understood resulting in expensive errors.
- Inconsistent, incompetent or lack of service from tax authorities Lack of time, expertise, and/or money for professional help.

You are not alone in your bewilderment or annoyance at the time-consuming task of the annual tax preparation routine. To ensure you probe well for the right answers and get the results you want from your relationship with the CRA, you need to tackle the tax return (we'll help you with that in later chapters) and then focus on managing after tax wealth throughout your lifetime. That's the big picture.

IN SUMMARY

THINGS YOU NEED TO KNOW

- Real wealth management is the after-tax, after-cost, and after-inflation result of accumulation, growth, preservation, and transition of wealth.

- Tax-efficiency is the skill of managing the dollars you make and save, so as to receive them first, keep them in your pocket longest, ultimately to pay the least possible tax as a family unit.

- Your MTR (Marginal Tax Rate) is a useful tool in measuring tax-efficiency on the next dollar you'll earn.

- Various income sources are subject to different marginal tax rates. You can diversify away "tax risk" by increasing the number of different sources of revenue you earn.

- Clawbacks on social benefits and tax credits can increase your marginal tax rate significantly.

- Tax-efficient investments, like the Registered Retirement Savings Plan (RRSP), can reduce your taxes and increase your eligibility for social benefits and tax credits, thereby reducing your marginal tax rate.

- Your Effective Tax Rate is the actual rate of tax you have paid on your total income: the end result of your tax astute game plan, before social benefits and refundable credits.

- Understanding the significant components of your tax return, ending with your effective tax rate will pave the way for you to focus on tax planning—the path to real wealth.

- Do what you're good at: if taxes are mystical to you, learn enough to ask deep probing questions about your after-tax results and pre-tax opportunities of your tax advisor. This book will help you do that.

QUESTIONS YOU NEED TO ASK[2]

- How much tax did I pay on my total income last year?
- How much tax will I pay in my lifetime? (Hint: multiply your actual taxes paid this year by the number of years you expect to work for an interesting approximation.)
- What is my effective tax rate?
- What is my marginal tax rate?
- What income sources should I be earning to maximize tax-efficiency?
- What tax-preferred investments will generate those tax results?
- How can I avoid or defer paying taxes in the future?
- How can I qualify for more tax deductions, credits, and social benefits?
- How can I build more "real wealth" for the future?

THINGS YOU NEED TO DO

- Make a commitment to learn more about your tax affairs.
- Consider learning how to use tax preparation software. It can help you prepare "What if" scenarios regarding income levels and income sources.
- Find an experienced tax practitioner to help you with your tax preparation and planning.
- Consider ways to do more of what you do best: use your skills to negotiate and plan for more tax-efficient income.
- Evaluate your relationship with your financial advisor. You need to add tax-efficiency to your discussion about portfolio construction, asset allocation, and wealth management strategies. Find someone who is equipped with the skills to do that with you.

---

[2] Ask the appropriate question of your tax, financial, and legal advisors.

DECISIONS YOU NEED TO MAKE

- Is wealth accumulation important to me?
- Is paying less tax important to me?
- Am I willing to invest time in learning how to reduce my taxes to build more wealth?
- Can I make the effort to be more organized about my tax documents?
- Do I have the discipline to spend less so I can invest with tax-efficiency?

If you answered yes to these questions, you are well on your way to mastering your taxes!

MASTER YOUR TAXES
The Big Picture

TIPS

Mastering your taxes is about overcoming two pain points: time and money. Take control of the first dollar you make by managing "tax leakage":

- Earn tax-efficient income.
- Resolve to pay less and to put more money in your pocket first.
- Understand the basic components of your tax return.
- Find out how to tap into more social benefits and tax credits from governments.
- Use an understanding of your effective and marginal tax rates to monitor improvements due to your tax planning.
- Diversify tax risk by earning income from a variety of sources.
- Commit to a tax-efficient investment plan to start building real wealth.
- Start a relationship with a team of professionals focused on your tax-efficiency.

TRAPS

- Don't be passive about the taxes: it's too expensive in the long run.
- Don't miss an opportunity to invest with tax-efficiency.
- Don't glaze over when it comes to tax terminology: master it or it will cost you.

Principle Mastery: Volatile market fluctuations that erode or enhance your investments will always be calmed with a tax-efficient approach. Focus on your ROI—Return on Investment—after tax.

CHAPTER 2

Change the Game: You, First

"I don't understand why anyone can just take my money—before I even see it!"

Jeannie, contemplating her first pay stub, was aghast: shocked, in fact, at the size of her tax withholdings. Having just graduated from university in the spring, she was delighted to take a high paying job as an assistant producer with a national media company. Her dream was to go to New York and work her way up the ranks as a foreign correspondent. "I'll never be able to live my dreams if I don't get to keep what I earn!"

Her mom, an accountant working out of her home office, looked up from her work with a meaningful nod of agreement. "Jeannie, you need to learn to pay yourself first. There are simple things you can do to pay less tax and keep more for you, the starting point is to take control of the first dollar you earn every week."

THE ISSUES

Those who have been in the workforce for a while understand that it's what you keep, not necessarily what you earn, that counts. Many outstretched hands will vie for a share of those earnings throughout your lifetime, but for most people the most prevalent benefactor will be the federal and provincial governments and, as Jeannie discovered, in most cases they get paid first.

Tax prepayment and overpayment is common to most employees, to their financial detriment. With so much coming off the top, they are often left spinning their financial wheels, never quite able to gain the traction they need to propel forward towards their financial goals.

Others are better positioned: they negotiate employment contracts that allow them to leverage the economic activity their productivity creates: they take home cash but also perks—benefits of employment that involve the use of their employer's dollars to make improvements to their lifestyle. This can include group health benefits or low interest loans for investment purposes for example.

Still other taxpayers receive all the money for their economic efforts. This provides them with the resources to meet needs, invest the balance, and then pay tax. These people are often the employers or investors in companies that employ others. *They have control of all the money, first.* Because of this they have essentially changed the game, sharing with themselves and their families first and the government second.

And that's the issue: by changing the game, and taking control of as much of your earnings *sooner* and for *longer*, you will not only be better able to fund needs and wants but able to build more wealth for your future too. Astute taxpayers take control of their gross earnings and leverage the combined economic power of both the employer and the employee.

THE SOLUTIONS

We have learned that individuals and their various income sources can be treated differently for tax purposes. That's true even though gross income levels may be similar one neighbor to the next. Those who retain more wealth—and therefore more freedom of choice over lifestyle—will benefit from a more vigilant approach to the time value of money, and maximize their take home pay.

What do we mean by this? Investopedia[1] describes the time value of money as follows:

> *"The idea that money available at the present time is worth more than the same amount in the future, due to its potential earning capacity. This core principle of finance holds that, provided money can earn interest, any amount of money is worth more the sooner it is received."*

Understanding the Time Value of Money[1] author Shauna Carther, makes a great point, succinctly describing why this is important to you in making financial decisions:

> *"Why would any rational person defer payment into the future when he or she could have the same amount of money now? For most of us, taking the money in the present is just plain instinctive. So at the most basic level, the time value of money demonstrates that, all things being equal, it is better to have money now rather than later…**time literally is money**—the value of the money you have now is not the same as it will be in the future and vice versa."*

So why do intelligent, hard working people willingly fork over 30%, 40%, and even 50% of their pay to the tax department—*people they don't even know*—every year with little complaint or fanfare, other than perhaps some frustration and resignation at the process? Why are they so willing to overpay those tax withholdings, just to get a refund at the end of the year, with no interest for the use of their money in the meantime?

---

[1] Investopedia.com; a Forbes Company, 2007

That's just not smart, especially when the solutions for getting more money into your pocket fast are easy and at your fingertips.

Here's what you need to do to meet your tax obligations and be first out of the starting gate, with the traction you need to meet your financial goals:

1. Take control of your gross earnings.
2. Diversify away tax risk.
3. Maximize your deductions.
4. Take a "lifecycle" approach to your tax planning.

TAKE CONTROL OF YOUR GROSS EARNINGS

When you started that first job and annually ever since, you may have been handed a series of tax forms to help your company's payroll department understand how much tax you wanted deducted from your gross pay.

This involves actually knowing about and indicating which "personal tax credits" you qualify for. Most people don't understand what this means, and looking from the incomprehensible tax terms on the forms, to their rushed payroll clerk, they are often given the following response to their "deer in the headlights" expression: *Just claim single; you'll owe nothing more at tax time.*

And with that advice, inferring of course that you may not be able to save any sum, let alone enough to pay your taxes, it becomes an accepted habit for life to overpay the taxes your employer deducts at "source", that is from your gross pay! Unfortunately, this is one of those decisions that can put you at great financial peril.

People would have a better chance of paying all of their bills and saving for their future if they weren't losing control of so much of their gross pay. In recent years the average tax refund is significant: over $1400, or $120 a month. This is money you essentially loan to the government without being paid any interest in return.

Put another way, it's like owning a rental property, having tenants and then not charging rent!

Over a 40 year working life, $1400 a year would grow to an accumulation of $56,000 before interest is earned. When you assume an average interest rate of 2% that money would grow to over $75,000—more than the average amount most people have in their RRSPs today.[2] Inside an RRSP, earning the same rate, that refund would grow to over $86,000. (Investing the same sum inside an RRSP at a 5% average rate of return, the money would grow to close to $180,000! You can see that interest rates and tax sheltering inside an RRSP matter a lot.)

It is clear that this average tax refund, invested in your hands instead of the government's, is extremely lucrative due to the basic effect of compounding over the lifetime of an average worker. *Change the game: pay only the correct amount of tax on your income sources by being in control of more of your employment earnings first.* Here's how:

Reduce your tax withholdings on your income sources; complete the forms, properly

To reduce your tax withholdings you'll be doing two things: first, telling the government about the personal tax credits you are entitled to in reducing your taxes. Second, you'll tell the government about certain allowable deductions you will have this year.

1. **The TD1 Personal Tax Credits.** One of these forms must be completed for the federal tax you'll pay and one for the provincial portion. The most common federal and provincial tax credits, used to reduce the amount of income subject to tax, are the following:

   Available to everyone
   - Basic Personal Amount (no receipts required!)
   - Charitable Donation Amounts (based on your contributions or asset transfers)

   For seniors
   - Age Amount, if you are 65 or over
   - Pension income amount

---

[2] The Wealth of Canadians 2005, Statistics Canada.

For families

- Spouse Amount
- Amount for Eligible Child (Equivalent-to-Spouse)
- Amount for Child under 18
- Amount for Infirm Adult
- Canada Fitness Amounts
- Public Transit Pass Amounts
- Amount for Adoption Expenses
- Tuition, education and textbook amount
- For Dependants who are sick or disabled:
- Caregiver Amount
- Disability Amount
- Medical Amounts (based on your income and expenses)

If you are filling in the TD1 forms for yourself, it is helpful to look back at your last federal tax return to see what you claimed on "Schedule 1", which lists credits you claimed last year. Will anything change for you or your family this year? Will you be getting married or divorced? Going back to school? Having a baby? Moving your sick aunt into your home for caregiving? All of these circumstances can result in extra reductions to your tax withholding requirements.

2. **The T1213: Request for a Reduction in Tax Withholdings.** Will you be spending money for any of the following expenses? If so, request that your tax withholdings be reduced. You'll get to keep more of the money you've made so that you can actually make these transactions:

- RRSP contributions
- Child care expenses
- Tax deductible spousal support payments
- Employment expenses like auto expenses, home office or cost of an assistant
- Costs associated with your investments like interest on your investment loans, also known as carrying charges

- Other significant tax deductible costs like moving expenses, medical expenses or charitable donations

Simply fill out the T1213 form, send it to the CRA, and they'll give your employer permission to reduce your taxes on your income source. Most people don't know about this and it can make a big difference in your ability to build wealth.

If you need help with any of this talk to the person who did your tax return, they can tell you the exact amounts for the current year. Most personal tax credits are adjusted for inflation every year, and so their values will change. Ideally you should revisit the personal amounts available to you at the end of the current year, in December, when the new forms for the next year are available and you have a chance to do some year end tax planning. Be sure to indicate every credit and deduction you think you'll be entitled to.

Recover Overpaid Instalments

Certain people have to pay income taxes by making instalment payments. For 2008 and subsequent years, to qualify for quarterly instalment payments taxes payable after you file your tax return must be over $3,000 for the current year or either of the prior two years. This can happen when taxpayers report income from self-employment, investments, or other sums from which tax is not withheld at source.

Farmers and fishers, will make one instalment payment by December 31, but only if the actual tax owing for either of the two preceding years does not exceed $3,000.

When taxpayers fall into an instalment profile, they will receive a regular billing notice from CRA reminding them about this, based on their taxes payable of the immediately prior two years. Trouble is, if income has fallen since then, instalments may no longer be necessary. Yet many people keep paying the request for instalments sent by the CRA, instead of using or investing that extra money for themselves.

Good news: you can request an adjustment to change your instalment remittances by writing a letter and requesting instalments be calculated under one of two other options:

- **Current-Year Option.** Under this option, the taxpayer's income tax liability (plus amounts that will be owing to the Canada Pension Plan—CPP) for the current taxation year is estimated, and then one-quarter of the estimated amount over $3000 is due on each of the four due dates: March 15, June 15, September 15 and December 15.

- **Prior-Year Option.** Under this option, you will estimate your instalments based on your prior year taxes and CPP premiums owing. Tax software computes this easily; otherwise see your tax professional for help.

Taking control of your gross earnings is the first step in controlling more of your money so that you can actually have the money to pay your bills and make investments, too. This is a much better way to manage your cash flow.

DIVERSIFY AWAY TAX RISK

People who work as employees are in a master-servant relationship with both their employers and the taxman. They leave control over where they work and how they work to their employer, who bears the risk of loss and supplies the assets required to work. The employer also must make tax payments on your behalf to governments, as mandated by law.

While the employer takes the risk for profits and loss, and invests in income-producing assets, he or she has control over all the money, first.

This is important. As an employee, you will want to tap into more of those available corporate tax dollars, which are bigger, because corporations pay less tax than individuals do.

Have Employer Dollars Fund Lifestyle

You will want to discover for example whether corporate tax dollars are available to fund your lifestyle. Some of these "perks" can be received tax-free, as indicated by the asterisk:

- employer-provided vehicles, their gas, oil, and car maintenance
- reimbursement for travel and home office costs
- private and company-funded pension benefits
- private group health care benefits and life insurance*
- education costs for courses taken to benefit the employer*
- membership to athletic clubs*
- reimbursements for meals and entertainment*
- discounts on merchandise*
- computers and communication devices*
- vacations that involve the employer's business (may be partially taxable)*
- home relocation loans, and reimbursement of moving expenses any losses on the principal residence if an employer-required move is required*
- financial counseling and income tax preparation services*
- death benefits: up to $10,000 can be received by your family on a tax-free basis to help pay for funeral costs*

Participate in Growth of Assets

Employees also want to be sure they can put themselves in a similar tax position as their employers, whose compensation can include salary, interest, dividends, or capital gains on the sale of their income-producing assets. These folks receive preferred tax treatment for taking risks, being able to claim all reasonable expenditures incurred to earn revenues. The employees who work for them want to leverage off that risk, as they are contributing to the growth of that equity too. You will want to see if it's possible to negotiate access to the following:

- incentive and performance bonuses
- stock options and profit sharing plans
- employer-provided loans for investment purposes

These benefits are taxable, but worthwhile, as they leverage the employer's resources.

Remember, these income sources attract different tax treatment, which gives you the opportunity to average down your marginal rate of tax.

Maximize Your Deductions

Unfortunately many employees are unaware that they may be able to claim out-of-pocket expenses incurred by virtue of their employment, on the tax return. To do so, it is necessary to keep Form T2200 *Declaration of Conditions of Employment*, signed by the employer, in your files in case of audit by CRA. The form states that these out of pocket expenses have not been reimbursed and are required under your contract of employment.

The tax savings on these deductions can be lucrative in some cases, freeing up new capital for investment purposes. Those who earn salary only may deduct the following out-of-pocket expenses:

- accounting and legal fees, not including income tax preparation.
- motor vehicle expenses (including Capital Cost Allowance (CCA), interest or leasing costs, as well as operating costs like gas and oil, maintenance and repairs, but only if the employee is not in receipt of a non-taxable allowance for the use of the car).
- travel expenses including rail, air, bus or other travel costs which take the employee outside the employer's metropolitan area.
- meals, tips, and hotel costs providing the excursion is for at least 12 hours and away from the taxpayer's metropolitan area. Only one half of meals and tips are claimable, though.
- parking costs (but generally not at the place of employment).
- supplies used up directly in your work (stationery, maps, teacher's supplies, etc.).
- office rent or certain home office expenses.
- new tool costs of certain tradespersons.

Employees who earn their living negotiating contracts for their employers or selling on commission may claim expenses for travel and sales costs, itemized below, if they are required to pay their own expenses, regularly perform their duties away from their employer's place of business, and do not receive a tax-free travel allowance.

- When travel expenses only are claimed, the amounts may exceed commissions earned and excess expenses over income may be used to offset other income of the year.

- Deductible sales expenses include promotional expenses, entertainment expenses (subject to the 50% restriction for personal consumption), travel, auto, and home office costs. *However*, expenses that exceed commissions earned in the calendar year may not be claimed except for interest and capital cost allowance on a motor vehicle.

For employees, deductible equipment costs are subject to special rules. Employees are not allowed to make a claim for assets like electronic equipment, but may purchase and deduct certain costs of vehicles, musical instruments or aircraft used for employment purposes. Therefore, it is wise tax planning to lease computers, or other required equipment.

Artists and musicians may claim expenses for items specific to their profession, including capital cost allowance on musical instruments.

Employees who work for employers who are in the business of transporting goods or services may be able to claim board and lodging expenses as well.

It can therefore pay to become more tax aware if you have out-of-pocket expenses relating to your employment.

Look For Opportunities to Split Income with Family Members

Employees who are required by their contract of employment to hire an assistant may deduct this cost. There is no rule that says this can't be paid to your spouse or child. Simply follow the same procedures you would to pay a stranger, and keep all records. The amounts must be reasonable, for work actually performed and the amounts must actually have been paid. Ask your tax advisor about making this claim audit-proof.

Don't Forget about the GST Rebate

Many employees who pay GST/HST on union or professional fees or employment expenses claimed on the tax return miss applying for a refund of GST paid on those deductible items. Do so when you file your personal tax return.

Secure Your Family's Future on Job Termination

Difficult times for your employer could result in your job terminated. When it is time to part ways, a severance package can provide for a soft landing and can suddenly boost your income into a highly-taxed top bracket. These packages are usually paid in a lump sum, but may be paid periodically. They are usually fully taxable, but may qualify for some tax breaks, with proper planning. Therefore the time to see your tax advisor about this is before you agree to take the money, to ensure you keep as much as possible after-tax. Know the following:

- For years of service prior to 1996, it is possible to "rollover" some of your severance on a tax-free basis to your RRSP. This is called the "eligible" retiring allowance. Check with your HR department to find out how much this is.

- Otherwise invest as much of your severance as you can into an RRSP, based on your unused RRSP contribution room. The will give you an offsetting tax deduction which may reduce the rate of tax you may need to pay.

- Negotiate to take your severance to be paid out over a couple of tax years, if that results in the income being subject to lower tax brackets and rates.

- Ask your payroll clerk to annualize the taxes withhold on your severance package—that is to calculate the taxes based on your annual income for the year with the bonus, rather than the top rate of tax this lump sum will likely attract in this pay period.

- You might qualify for a lump sum averaging calculation to be applied over three years to try to minimize the tax bite. Ask your tax advisor about this.

- If you fight your employer under a wrongful dismissal suit, legal fees might be tax deductible once you settle.

- Try to negotiate a continuation of group health and insurance benefits. If the employer is not in agreement, ask for the components of the plan that are convertible to you to be transferred, so that you can continue the premiums personally if that is to your benefit.

Rather than a termination, it may be possible to negotiate a "phased-in retirement" that allows you to work part time, while you tap into benefits from your employer-funded pension plan. This new opportunity has been available for employees who are at least age 55 starting in 2008.

Unfunded Pension Plans

In recent difficult times, employees have been worried about whether their employer-funded pension plan will result in a pension benefit. There is no doubt that the financial crisis of 2008 deepened those worries. Senior analysts at Standard & Poor's[3] predicted that even if equity markets remain flat for the remainder of 2008, defined benefit plans may end up with a combined under-funding well in excess of the record $219 billion experienced in 2002.

As a result, underfunding poses a significant threat to current and future pension receivers. If your employer offers an employer-sponsored pension plan, it is important to understand the terms of the plan, its ability to pay a benefit, and what happens to your portion of the funding if it cannot.

We will discuss retirement planning and the tax advantages offered by registered pension plans in particular as it relates to income splitting opportunities later in this book. If things don't turn out quite the way you plan, you'll be glad you focused on your taxes, and the time value of money, to generate as much capital as possible along the way. In bad times, all savings count.

---

[3] Standard and Poor's is a leading source for credit ratings, indices, investment research, risk evaluation and data.

Consider Self-Employment

Many find themselves in a new position after the termination of their employment: self-employment. For many this can prove to be a masterful career move. Learn more about the tax efficiencies of self-employment later in this book...a great way to diversify income and manage risk.

TAKE A "LIFECYCLE" APPROACH TO YOUR TAX PLANNING

The majority of Canadians will die in old age—that is after age 65. Most will qualify for some type of public pensions, such as Old Age Security or the Canada Pension Plan. Most will also want to supplement those public sources with personal savings, to cope with unknowns like taxes and inflation.

Do you need to worry about that at age 24? Not really, but if you understand the time value of money, and resolve to pay only the correct amount of tax—no more—throughout your lifetime, you will be able to focus on the benefits of long term investing, with more money, sooner. Your future financial success can be guaranteed if you consistently save some portion of every dollar you make along the way. A tax-efficient strategy to do so will help.

It is the young that have the most potential to accumulate the wealth. They have time on their hands to weather economic cycles, they can work and invest longer, so their recovery time is better. They will likely inherit money and capital and they will benefit from the time value of money: the number of years they have to reinvest the money they earn.

Consider the following lifeline approach to your tax planning, which can help you ask the right questions of your advisors. You will learn more about the powerful opportunities for income splitting with families, in our next chapter.

A TAX-EFFICIENT LIFECYCLE

AGE	TAX PLANNING MILESTONES
Birth	• Open savings account to invest Universal Child Care Benefit. Resulting earnings are taxed in the hands of the child. • Open a non-registered account for transfers of capital.
Under 7	• Increased child care expense deductions and Child Tax Benefits.
0-17	• Invest in Registered Education Savings Plans and earn Canada Education Savings Grants and Learning Bonds. • File tax returns if the child has earned income to build up RRSP contribution room. • A "kiddie tax" may apply to certain earnings from private corporations. • The child is a dependant for the purpose of Canada Pension Plan disability and survivor benefits. • The child is a dependant child for the purposes of the Child Amount.
Age 15	• Last year for eligibility for the Canada Fitness Tax Credit and child care expense claims (unless disabled). • May qualify for education amount only if courses are taken at a post-secondary level.
Age 17	• File a tax return to claim the refundable GST Credit and create room to make contributions to a TFSA—Tax-Free Savings Account.
Age 18	• Eligibility to contribute to the Canada Pension Plan. • Eligibility to open a TFSA. • Contributions to a Registered Disability Savings Plan are based on beneficiary's income. • Transfer tuition, education and textbook credits to parents, grandparents or spouse. • A $2000 over contribution to an RRSP is allowed.
Age 21	• Income earned on deposits of personal injury awards become taxable.
Age 31	• Age eligibility for contribution to an RESP ends.

AGE	TAX PLANNING MILESTONES
Age 35	• Age eligibility for contribution to an RESP ends for a disabled beneficiary.
Age 49	• Registered Disability Savings Grant and Bond eligibility ends.
Age 18 to 55	• Earning and investing years: file a tax return every year. • Invest in a TFSA every year. • Make RRSP contributions every year. • Open non-registered accounts for other surplus savings. • Buy a tax exempt principal residence. • Manage debt and interest costs. • Grow your personal net worth.
Age 55	• Eligibility for a phased in retirement: take company pension early.
Age 59	• Eligibility for contribution to a Registered Disability Savings Plan ends.
Age 60	• Eligibility for early withdrawal of Canada Pension Plan Benefits.
Age 65	• Old Age Security benefits begin; eligibility for Age Amount. • Canada Pension Plan Benefits. • In home caregiver amounts may be claimable. • Conversion of RPPs and RRSPs to pension benefits.
Age 70	• Last year for contributing to the Canada Pension Plan.
Age 71	• Conversion of RRSP to RRIF or annuity; maturation of deferred profit sharing plans.
Age 90-100	• Maximum RRIF payout age, terms of several types of annuities end.

IN SUMMARY

Living independently requires the funding of both needs and wants in the short term, while achieving peace of mind about your financial future. Against the backdrop of life's uncertainties—job loss, volatile investment returns, disability, divorce, and the timing of retirement and death—significant financial risk can be diversified away with tax planning.

To pay yourself first, you have to change the game. Stop sending the government so much of your money in advance. Never give up control over your money or how you earn it. Remember, real wealth is what you are left with after tax, inflation, and costs: your true purchasing power for the lifestyle you want, now and in the future.

THINGS YOU NEED TO KNOW

- Tax prepayment and overpayment is common to most employees.
- Holding more of your money sooner and for longer can help you build more wealth.
- The time value of money should work in your favor, not the government's.
- By minimizing tax withheld at source, taxpayers have more money to fund wants and needs and invest for the future.
- Diversifying income sources can help you pay a lower average tax.
- Negotiate employment contracts that feature both wages and benefits.
- Try to participate in the growth of your employer's business.
- Invest using a low interest loan from your employer if possible.
- Write off out-of-pocket expenses incurred to earn income from employment on your tax return.
- Hire your spouse or child to help you earn your income.
- Secure your future on job termination: plan to keep more of your severance package after tax.
- See the big picture: a lifecycle of tax-efficient opportunities for your time and money.

QUESTIONS YOU NEED TO ASK

- What can I do to reduce my tax withholding at source?
- How can I increase my tax deductible expenses—and reduce my taxes withheld at source even more?
- How can I diversify the income I receive from employment?
- What taxable and tax-free benefits might I qualify to receive from my employer?
- Should I contribute to both the company pension plan and my RRSP?
- How can I minimize taxes payable on my severance package?
- What are the significant tax filing milestones I need to be aware of throughout my lifetime?

THINGS YOU NEED TO DO

- Complete your TD1 form by correctly identifying your personal tax credits.
- Further reduce your withholding taxes by filing Form T1213 to request a reduction to take into account other deductions and credits available.
- Change your instalment payment plan to eliminate quarterly payments.
- Renegotiate your employment contract to be more tax-efficient.
- Try to leverage your corporate employer's bigger after-tax dollars by negotiating an interest free loan, sponsorship of your education, or use of a car, etc.
- Don't rely solely only on the employer's pension plan. Save for your own retirement too.

DECISIONS YOU NEED TO MAKE

- Do I have a game plan for maximizing the time value of my money?
- Should I reduce my tax refund to use more of my gross pay sooner?
- Should I invest this new money in an RRSP?
- Should I claim my unreimbursed, out-of-pocket expenses of employment?
- Can I diversify my compensation to minimize tax and benefit from perks?
- Do I know how much retirement income my company pension plan will pay me?
- Is it possible to protect the erosion of my severance package from tax?
- Am I aware of significant tax filing milestones to get the results I want when speaking with my tax professional?

If you answered yes to these questions, you are already on your way to changing the game in your favour by mastering control of more of your earnings to work for you in accumulating wealth. If you answered no, you have some work to do with your tax and financial advisors.

MASTER YOUR TAXES
Change the Game: You, First

TIPS

- Envision the financial decisions you need to make to achieve your goals.
- Some of those decisions will be driven by milestones initiated by the tax system.
- Most people start their career working as employees, in a master-servant relationship. There are few tax advantages to this structure.
- Employees can, however, benefit from their employer's resources.
- By diversifying income sources you may be able to gain access to more dollars or benefits sooner, and taxed at lower rates.
- Make it your business to reduce employment income with your allowable out-of-pocket expenditures.
- It is important to keep and invest more of your earnings by paying only the correct amount of tax, but no more.
- Take control and invest your tax refund.
- An RRSP contribution is a good first choice, if you have accumulated the required RRSP contribution room.

TRAPS

- Never overpay taxes withheld on income sources.
- Many people pay big money for financial advisors to properly construct and monitor investment portfolios, only to undo that fine work by cashing in investments at the wrong time to fund tax instalments they may not need to make. Never overpay your quarterly instalments.
- Employees may not benefit from the sale of a business asset, built with their input. Consider how you can participate in building equity for yourself with your investments.

Principle Mastery: Master your taxes by taking control of your before-tax earnings. Change the game to pay yourself first. Fund your lifestyle by leveraging your relationship with both your employer and the taxman. If you can, consider self-employment in your income diversification strategy.

CHAPTER 3

Family Next: Powerful Income Splitting Opportunities

To put the world right in order, we must first put the nation in order; to put the nation in order, we must first put the family in order; to put the family in order, we must first cultivate our personal life; we must first set our hearts right. CONFUCIUS

"I want to share my life with you," Tom spoke softly as he slipped the wedding ring on his bride's finger. "With this ring, I thee wed."

Tom and Kathy had lived together for two years. Now after many lovely experiences, they were ready to commit to each other in front of their friends and family, and declare the start of their own nuclear family unit. They looked forward to their first home, their first child, and their future.

Kathy looked back on that lovely day as she checked "married" for the first time on her personal tax return. How things had changed since they wed: her career as a marketing consultant had prospered; Tom's was in a slump. He was concerned about losing his job as a manager at a local manufacturing plant. Thank goodness they had each other and the power of two incomes, two investment accounts, and two pensions to average their fortunes through good years and bad.

CHAPTER 3 ✦ FAMILY NEXT: POWERFUL INCOME SPLITTING OPPORTUNITIES 43

THE ISSUES

Are married people in fact wealthier? Indeed, and there are several reasons for this. American authors, Linda Waite and Maggie Gallagher[1], found this in their research on why married people are wealthier:

> *"It takes only 1.5 times as much money to support two people living together as it would if they lived apart. Knowing this provides an additional temptation to cohabit. But cohabiting couples seldom accumulate wealth in the same way that married couples do. They are far more tentative about their relationship; less inclined to invest together in homes, stocks and furniture; and more likely to do such things as keep separate bank accounts and take separate vacations.*
>
> *On the verge of retirement, the typical married couple has accumulated a total of about $410,000—or $205,000 for each person—as compared to $167,000 for the never married, $154,000 for the divorced, $151,000 for the widowed and just under $96,000 for the separated."*

The same research holds true in Canada. In *The Wealth of Canadians: An Overview of the Survey of Financial Security 2005*[2], it was found that:

- Single income married couples and lone-parent single males earned the highest average income in Canada at $54,900. Single males earned 64% of that income; single females only 53%. Singles are also less prepared for retirement: Single individuals had only 27% the private pension assets couples without children had, and only 52% of assets accumulated by couples with children.

- 30% of family units had no private pension assets; most of these were headed by single parents.

Education matters, *a lot* in building a financially secure future. Specifically, those with a university degree or other post-secondary certificate had the highest median net worth while those with less than a high school education had the lowest.

---

[1] *The Case for Marriage: Why Married People Are Happier, Healthier and Better Off Financially*, Doubleday 2000.

[2] By Pensions and Wealth Surveys Section of Statistics Canada, released in September 2007.

Know that despite the fact that it is individuals that are taxed on their world income in Canada, *it is families that make the most powerful economic decisions as a unit.* It seems to pay to find a great partner, get an education, and then save for your family's future by mentoring great family relationships and keeping family wealth intact.

It becomes clear that preparedness for a financially independent life is important for each individual in the family, and that the right education can help. When you add a tax-efficient approach to those decisions, and all the tax benefits the government provides to support families, you have a winning strategy for success in financial decision making as an economic unit.

There's much to learn, however, to take advantage of the opportunities. The challenge for most seems to be, how to start...

THE SOLUTIONS

Mastering your taxes has never been more important in light of the global credit crunch. Against the backdrop of significant losses to personal portfolios, pensions and housing valuations, tax-efficiency has become more important than ever to families.

It becomes clear from the statistics on wealth accumulation, that once people gain some financial traction and acquire some capital, they are able to grow and preserve their wealth much more significantly: households with $500,000 plus in investable assets held 57% of all household wealth in Canada. When you accumulate as a family, you have numerous tax savings opportunities single people don't have. We will look at many of these in later chapters as we discuss career, home ownership, investment, retirement and tax planning. However, any discussion about tax planning for families must first involve an understanding of the following:

- Who is "married" for tax purposes?
- How can we master family tax filing opportunities?
- How can we combine resources to save more?
- In what ways can we preserve family capital?
- Is it possible to use tax planning to help with the credit crunch?

WHO IS "MARRIED" FOR TAX PURPOSES?

Family structure is complicated today. Conjugal relationships—legal or common law—require the combining, reporting, and sharing of financial resources under provincial marital property laws and for certain provisions of the Income Tax Act. Who is "married" for tax purposes? Do common law unions count? How long do you have to live together for tax purposes? How do your "live-ins" affect your eligibility for social benefits and tax credits?

Here's what you need to know about the tax status of your relationships:

- Check "married" on your tax return if you are legally married, whether you are a heterosexual or same sex couple.
- Check "common law" if you have lived together with your partner for a continuous period of 12 months or if at December 31 you were parents of a natural or adoptive child together. Common law couples are treated like married couples for tax purposes.
- Check "separated" if you have been apart for a period of 90 days or more, or you have a written separation agreement.
- Check "divorced" if you have dissolved your marriage with a court order or decree.
- Check "widowed" if you lost your spouse or common-law partner to death during the year.

These various conjugal relationships affect the filing of tax returns significantly, for example:

- They can increase or decrease your monthly cash intake from Child Tax Benefits.
- Maximize your opportunities to contribute to investments like RRSPs.
- They can help you maximize the use of each family member's personal "tax-free zones" by transferring certain credits between spouses, or win on pension income splitting if you are a couple receiving benefits from one partner's company pension plan.
- They can also restrict you to having just one tax exempt personal residence for your family unit.

In terms of the tax preparation process, this requires a family focus, rather than individual, for the best tax advantages for the family unit as a whole. Immerse yourself in that process later in this book, but for now understand that the family that files tax returns together wins more in tax savings. Mastering your taxes as a family will result in bigger resources for wealth creation.

HOW CAN WE MASTER TAX FAMILY TAX FILING OPPORTUNITIES?

A key element in minimizing taxes and maximizing wealth for a family is learning to think about tax planning from the perspective of the family unit as a whole rather than from the perspective of the individual family members. This is more complicated than it seems because in general we tax individual income in Canada; there is no joint filing of returns. Yet, there are provisions that allow for income splitting between spouses, sharing of certain tax deductions and credits, and the comparison of family net income for the purposes of leveraging refundable and non-refundable tax credits.

In short, the Canadian tax system is a hybrid of provisions for individuals and family units. You really need to know the ropes to master your opportunities.

We have previously discussed the importance of paying yourself first. The process of maximizing your opportunity for a higher gross pay each month begins with vigilance over your tax withholdings. In addition, you have learned that as income rises, eligibility for refundable tax credits like the Child Tax Benefit, or social benefits like the Old Age Security can be "clawed back". The former is based on *family net income*, the latter on *individual net income*. Therefore, we need to keep an eye on the size of net income—line 236 of the tax return—for all adults in the family. This begins with the filing of your annual tax return.

To file family tax returns most advantageously takes a specific methodology you may not be familiar with. You will want to:

1. Prepare each return separately to the individual's best tax benefit, starting with the lowest income earner and working your way up

2. Look at the results on each return from a family, rather than individual, point of view

3. Tweak the returns, to claim the best tax results for the family unit as a whole, maximizing transferrable options for income, deductions, and credits.

4. Make decisions about acquiring tax-reducing investments—most commonly RRSPs—to reduce net income of some or all family members, so that you can benefit from more of the provisions available to you from CRA.

Following are some examples of provisions that may be split or transferred between spouses, providing for greater tax-efficiency for the family unit. Discuss these with your tax professional every year, especially if things have changed in your personal life, to make sure you are claiming all benefits you are entitled to, as a family.

- Income
  - Retirement benefits from the Canada Pension Plan
  - Periodic payments from company-sponsored retirement benefits or superannuation
  - Dividends, if the transfer results in an increased tax credit for your spouse
  - Salary or wages for assistance with certain employment income sources and as an employee or contractor to a proprietorship
- Deductions
  - Contributions to spousal RRSPs
  - Moving expenses
  - Child care costs under certain circumstances
  - Northern residents deductions
- Credits (Federal Non-Refundable)
  - Pension income amount
  - Age amount for those who have reached age 65 in the year
  - Amount (Credit) for child under 18

- Children's fitness amount
- Public transit amount
- Adoption amount
- Tuition, education and textbook amounts
- Disability amount
- Caregiver amount
- Amount for infirm dependants over 18
- Medical expenses
- Charitable donations
- Political contributions
- (Refundable)
  - Most refundable tax credits can be claimed by either spouse and are based on net family income. Federally these include the Child Tax Benefit, GST Credit, and the Working Income Tax Benefit. Some provinces feature provincial refundable credits too.

If you find you have missed using any of these provisions in past returns, you can go back and recover missed refunds due to your errors or omissions. We will explain how to do this under the *Taxpayer Relief Provision* in later chapters. That's important, because knowing you have maximized all your tax compliance provisions will position you to master your real wealth accumulations with larger after-tax dollars.

Also see the checklist of tax provisions to discuss with your advisor in the final chapter of this book.

HOW CAN WE COMBINE FAMILY RESOURCES TO SAVE MORE?

As income rises, so do tax rates and surtaxes. Generally, but depending on income source, it can be assumed that one person earning $40,000 will pay more tax than two people earning $20,000 each, or four family members earning $10,000 each. (Those lucky four will in fact pay no tax, as the Basic Personal Amount—or tax-free zone for each person— is $10,100 in 2009).

For these reasons, it may make sense to transfer income from the higher earners in the family to the lower to get better results for the family unit. You can also take advantage of the ability to shift tax, where possible, to other related taxpayers (i.e. family members) who are in a lower marginal tax bracket. Another strategy is to use a variety of alternative structures to split and averaging income.

CRA allows family income splitting in only limited circumstances. Otherwise, the *"Attribution Rules"* will thwart transfers of income and capital to family members. More about that later. For now, the goal is to consider a team approach in maximizing resources to accumulate more wealth.

Use a Team Approach

Tax-efficient family investing links tax strategies and investment strategies into an overall plan that leverages income, capital, tax preferences, and a variety of tax filing profiles. The end result of the tax-efficiency approach is to identify and employ more surplus or unused capital for investment, to create increased income for lifestyle needs and wants, and security for the future.

Tax-efficient investing is a way of linking tax advisory issues with the expertise of investment and financial advisors. A Tax-Efficient Investment Income Strategy is the bridge between investing activities and their after-tax results. It is important that investors on both the tax and the investment team understand the link between the two and proactively make decisions with you to get the best after-tax results over the long run.

Use Alternative Tax Structures

In some families, taxation extends beyond the individual and the family unit to "alternative taxpayers". These "alternative taxpayers" can provide a way to split and defer income and protect capital when wealth is transitioned. When a taxpayer dies this can also include elective T1 tax returns for certain types of income.

You may want to ask your professional team—tax practitioners, financial, and legal advisors about these options:

- The use of family trusts
- The use of operating and holding companies
- The use of personal and corporately owned insurance

IN WHAT WAYS CAN WE PRESERVE FAMILY CAPITAL?

We can plan to shift income, capital, and other taxes to lower earners in the family in a variety of ways. Every family investment planning strategy follows the same basic pattern: first review results for each individual in the family, then the results for the family must be considered. Discuss the following with your tax advisor:

- Identify current marginal tax rate for all family members.
- Identify taxable income sources realized during the year by each member of the family.
- Identify anticipated marginal tax rates for each different income source earned.
- Discuss ways to capitalize on personal tax-free zones, differences in types of income earned, the tax brackets to which income is subject to tax, and the related marginal tax rates.

Where income that would be taxed currently at a high marginal rate (example, fully taxable payments from a Registered Retirement Savings Plan) can be deferred until a later year when the marginal tax rate would be lower. The tax advantages can be significant, particularly when you view that opportunity within the context of the family unit. Where the amounts can be split between family members, results can often be even better.

Income Sources That Can Be Split

Recently governments have been moving towards family income splitting in very limited circumstances. For example, in 2007 it became possible for those who receive certain pension benefits to transfer up to 50% of that income to a spouse if that is to their tax advantage. This will usually provide for tax savings as pensioners take advantage of the progressivity of tax brackets and rates.

It is also possible for business owners to split the revenues they earn by hiring their spouse or children in the business, if they otherwise would have hired a stranger to perform the role. The family member must be qualified to perform the role and actually do so, for reasonable compensation similar to what would be paid to a stranger. In this case, the amounts paid are deductible to the business owner and taxable in the hands of the family member.

This is great tax planning, as it opens up tax advantaged investment opportunities for the family members by creating "room" for contributions to Registered Retirement Savings Plans (RRSP) and in the case of adults, contributions to the Canada Pension Plan (CPP), and Tax-Free Savings Account (TFSA).

Certain employed commission sales agents may also split income by hiring a family member as an assistant, however the fact that this assistance is required and paid for by the agent must be a condition of their contract of employment.

When it comes to splitting investment income the rules are more complicated, as described below. Passive income from investments is reported each calendar year and, with the exception of rental income, will not create RRSP contribution room. The primary categories of investment income are:

- **Interest:** this income is reported in full in the year received, or in the case of compounding investments, in the year accrued.
- **Dividends from Canadian Corporations:** Paid out after-tax profits of a corporation, the actual amounts received are "grossed up" on the tax return, thereby increasing a taxpayer's net income. You'll

see this on your T-slip as the "taxable" amount. This gross-up can have an effect on the size of refundable or non-refundable tax credits. However, the dividend is offset by a dividend tax credit which reduces federal taxes and, in the end, gives most investors better tax results than interest earnings. Dividends from Canadian Controlled Private Corporations are subject to different gross-up and dividend tax credit rates from those of public corporations, because of the way the corporations are taxed. This system integrates the personal and corporate tax systems in an attempt to avoid double taxation.

- **Rents:** This income is reported on a "net profit basis" and is generally nil, as many taxpayers like to reduce their rental income by claiming a deduction called Capital Cost Allowance based on the value of their building. This may however cause a tax problem in the future, if buildings appreciate over time.

- **Royalties:** This income is reported in full, but certain resource properties may be subject to more advantageous tax treatment.

It is important to understand how you might earn these types of income from your investments. If you are still unclear about these terms speak to your advisors so that you can match investment products to income sources.

Notice that capital gains earned on the sale of income producing assets, such as publicly traded shares or a rental property, are not included in this list of investment income sources. A capital gain occurs when an income producing asset is sold for more than its "adjusted cost base". That's your original acquisition value or price plus certain additions or deductions. Only one half of any capital gains are taxable, after you reduce them by any capital losses incurred during the year. This source is in a category by itself.

Circumventing Attribution Rules

When assets are transferred to family members, special rules exist to deny the opportunity of income splitting. In effect, any earnings from the transferred property are attributed back to the transferor. Here are the rules:

- **Property transferred between spouses is subject to attribution:** If the higher earner transfers property to the lower earner for investment purposes, resulting income from the investment is taxed in the hands of the transferor. Exceptions include:
  - Tax-Free Savings Account contributions.
  - Registered Disability Savings Plan (RDSP) contributions
  - Spousal RRSP contributions.
  - Income resulting from transactions in which bona fide "inter-spousal" loans are drawn up to transfer the capital and interest is actually paid to the lender at least once a year during the year or within 30 days after the year end.
  - Profits resulting from investments in a business, as described above.
  - Transfers resulting from marriage breakdown.
  - Income on property after it is inherited.
- **Property transferred to minor children:** Income in the form of dividends and interest will be attributed back to the transferor, however capital gains will be taxed in the hands of the minor.

  In addition, a "tax on split income", will be applied if minors receive dividends from private corporations owned by their parents. This "kiddie tax" also applies to income paid to minors from a trust or partnership, and cancel the advantage of income splitting.

  Other exceptions to the Attribution Rules on transfers of capital to minors include:
  - Contributions to TFSAs, RRSPs, and RESPs.
  - Any income earned on the investment of Child Tax Benefits or Universal Child Care Benefits in an account held in trust for the child.
  - Employment income actually earned by a child working in a parent's business.
- **Property transferred to adult children:** There are no restrictions on the type of property that can be transferred to adult children, and all resulting income will be taxed in their hands except if the

tax department believes the main reason for the loan was to reduce or avoid taxes by including the income on the adult child's return. The rules will not apply if:

- Amounts transferred are used for non-taxable investments: in a TFSA for example, principal residence, in the costs of education, car purchases, and so on.
- Contributions are made to the child's RRSP, RESP, or RDSP[3].
- A bona fide investment loan is drawn up, with interest actually paid at least once a year within 30 days after year-end, similar to inter-spousal loans.
- Transferred funds are used to start the child's business.

Recent tough times may provide a golden opportunity to transfer assets—like the family cottage—to adult children, given low market values. This should be discussed with your tax and legal advisor.

You should now have a good understanding of how to move income and capital around to family members to get more advantageous after tax results. Now, you need to know how to minimize risk during a credit crunch, using tax planning options available to you.

USE TAX PLANNING TO HELP YOUR FAMILY WITH THE CREDIT CRUNCH

When mom told you to save for a rainy day, she was right, and this might be it. If you aren't positioned for six to eight months of "safety cash" during a period of financial turmoil—whether by external forces or changes within your family structure—now is the time to put that in place.

Taxpayers can suffer financially when credit becomes scarce or more expensive. This can happen when you lose a job or business, or when the economic environment around you changes, as we have seen recently. You might find yourself sitting on an investment loan, margin account or mortgage that was affordable a few months ago, but no longer is.

---

[3] Registered Retirement Savings Plan, Registered Education Savings Plan, or Registered Disability Savings Plan.

It's often a good idea to look to the tax system to see if there are any provisions that can help you create new money fast. In fact, there are several to consider and discuss with your tax and financial advisors:

- **Need fast cash?** Unfiled tax returns, errors, or omissions on prior returns leading to refunds should be brought up to date.

- **Avoid overpaying tax instalments:** Can you avoid making quarterly instalment payments? Ask your professional to write CRA a letter to change your obligations. Your smooth relationship with CRA will be discussed in detail in later chapters.

- **Defer income:** Put off taking income until next year, to minimize tax and instalment payments. Seniors should stop drawing money from their Registered Retirement Income Funds if minimum withdrawal requirements have been met.

- **Take advantage of tax losses:** Whether you panicked and locked in losses, or generated them as part of your year end planning strategies, check out your cash flow advantages by carrying back losses to offset gains you may have reported in the previous three tax years.

- **Get your investment priorities right:** Don't cash in RRSPs if you can help it—this will cause a tax problem. Instead try to invest into an RRSP and generate cash with tax savings. Then decide: what investment should be made next: the new Tax-Free Savings Account or Registered Education Savings Plans (RESPs)?

- **Reconsider your charitable donations:** You can often generate fast cash on your tax return by increasing donations before year end. This includes the tax-free transfer of securities to your favorite charity. That donation receipt could create or increase your refund.

- **Increase social benefit payments:** Reducing your net income with an RRSP contribution, could decrease Old Age Security (OAS), clawbacks, and increase Child Tax Benefits. In both cases you'll have a monthly cash flow bonus.

- **Manage the credit crunch with deductible interest:** Know your options when you are in trouble: find out if and how to deduct interest costs for loans taken on assets with diminished value (ie. Stocks which values have crashed with the bear market), CRA garnishees, foreclosures, repossessions. Get rid of "bad debt" like expensive and non-deductible personal credit card balances. Get professional help.

- **Stress happens—write off your medical treatments:** Find yourself getting extra therapeutic massages, taking more prescription drugs? Do you know what medical expenses to write off? Keep all receipts; most prescribed medical expenditures are claimable on your return, if they are otherwise unreimbursed.

IN SUMMARY

THINGS YOU NEED TO KNOW

- Families are in a position to make the most powerful economic decisions as a unit and build more significant wealth than single people.
- When you include the potential for tax deductions, credits, and benefits available to families, the tax system can participate positively in your family's wealth creation.
- Conjugal relationships can vary from legally married to common law, and these rules can affect how benefits are applied for, tax returns are filed, and assets are held.
- Filing returns together as a family has advantages, particularly if you start with the lowest earner. Many transferrable provisions between family members may apply.
- By using the power of several individuals' tax-free zones and the progressive nature of our taxation system, a family unit can plan to pay less tax overall than individuals alone.
- High marginal tax rates, resulting from "clawbacks" of certain government benefits and credits, can be reduced when a family splits income.
- Alternative taxing structures, like family trusts and corporate accounts, may also serve to average taxes downward for the family.
- The Attribution Rules can provide a barrier to transferring funds from higher earners to lower earners, however, they can be circumvented by applying certain procedures.
- Reducing tax withholdings, instalments, and recovering missed refunds due to errors or omissions on prior-filed returns can help you create more cash, quickly.

QUESTIONS YOU NEED TO ASK

- What are the tax advantages of living as spouses—married or common law?
- What tax provisions can my spouse and I use jointly or transfer between us?
- What income sources should my spouse and I split?
- Who should be claiming the medical expenses and charitable donations?
- Should we consider making a spousal RRSP contribution?
- How can I transfer capital to my spouse or child?
- Can I transfer my losses to my spouse?
- Will a family trust help our family control more wealth?
- Should income from our rental business be reported on both spouses' returns?
- Who should report interest from savings in a joint account?
- How should we fund the deposit to the TFSA for my wife and adult child?
- How can I convert "bad debt" into "good, tax deductible debt"?

THINGS YOU NEED TO DO

- File tax returns with a family focus.
- Speak to your tax and financial advisors about the questions above.
- Make a plan to maximize family tax benefits and investments.

DECISIONS YOU NEED TO MAKE

- Whether your current financial advisors can help you with tax and investment planning.
- How to fund more investments for each family member.
- How to transfer more income to lower earners.

MASTER YOUR TAXES
Family Next: Powerful
Income Splitting Opportunities

TIPS

- Create enough taxable income each year for every individual in the family to use up their Basic Personal Amount or "tax-free zone".
- Invest money in a new Tax-Free Savings Account for adults in the family.
- File a tax return for everyone who has active income from employment or self-employment to create unused "RRSP contribution room". This can include young entrepreneurs with snow shoveling or baby-sitting businesses.
- Reduce family net income to maximize Child Tax Benefits and other refundable credits.
- Plan investments to build a powerful family legacy. Start with a disciplined, annual, non-negotiable investment approach using tax-preferred investments like RRSPs and TFSAs.
- Try to split income with family members to reduce average tax.

TRAPS

- Failure to file tax returns as a family can compromise available tax advantages.
- When families miss out on a group tax focus, average taxes will be higher.
- Only half as much wealth will be accumulated when investments are held outside of RRSP or TFSA accounts. Plan the order of your investments carefully.
- Intact family units are, statistically, wealthier than lone earners. Choose your life partner wisely.

Principle Mastery: Family tax and investment planning will help you accumulate more wealth by paying less in tax, receiving more in family benefits and maximizing the opportunity to build capital. There is tax assistance for those who want to accumulate wealth.

CHAPTER 4

Master the Process:
Tackling the Tax Return

A fine is a tax for doing wrong. A tax is a fine for doing something right.
UNKNOWN

> *"I'm just not that sure I want to be employed again," sighed Sarah, after receiving her third career notice about a company cut-back. "I've been around the block several times with these company reorgs and closures, and I think I just need to have control of my future."*
>
> *Sarah's husband, Jon completely agreed. "I've never been happier than since I started my consulting company, as you know. I'm in control of my money, how I make it and where it comes from."*
>
> *Sarah raised her eyebrows towards her husband in surprise. Hers had been the "safety income", and she was concerned he might think they have 'too many eggs in one basket' if she does not secure a job. "So you would support my decision, even though it would mean putting out time and money first and taking on some risk?"*
>
> *"Absolutely, smiled her husband in response. "I believe in you, dear."*

THE ISSUES

Do you believe in yourself? That's the issue for many people as jobs come and go, and career paths change. Today it is not unusual for people to be both employed and self-employed at the same time and that, in fact, may be a masterful career move; one that diversifies your risk when someone else has control of your future.

In today's world, achieving peace of mind is about taking control of your financial future. There is no doubt that being self-employed requires that risk capital and sweat equity be expended first. To be astute in business requires meticulous planning and solid focus on your clients and your goals. You need to put your resources of time and money on the line, together with your best problem solving skills. Many a 'successful' business person will smile at later accolades from those who only see the end result, but not the difficult and meager beginnings. It takes astute planning skills—and a good measure of luck—to nurture and grow your business from one stage to another.

But, it takes a savvy approach to understand that the operation of a business is really just another way to multiply the "buckets" in which to earn and save money on a tax-efficient basis. An important issue in the relationship with CRA, one that changes significantly when the taxpayer is self-employed. There are a variety of structures the company can operate within—proprietorship, partnership or corporation—but what is common to each is that the government must rely on your self-assessment, so the onus of proof for all the income and expenditures, and why you have made them in the way you have is on you, too.

Every business owner must be prepared to manage this relationship with CRA closely. The first step is a more focused investment in the structure and reporting of your fiscal activities. The second, a firm handle on your journey to fiscal success, something you should begin with the end in mind.

THE SOLUTIONS

There are definitely tax advantages to self-employment, whether that is under an unincorporated structure or an incorporated one. The activities of the business create revenues, which are deposited into business bank accounts first. The customers and their repeated buying and referrals build equity. And your astute management of resources can create significant real wealth.

In a corporate setting, it is not unusual for the owner-manager to be an employee of the company. Many family members may also be on the payroll or subcontract to it. Often those wages or independent contracts are funded by operating loans, upon which interest is tax deductible, and/or the pooling of equity the family members have saved. Income and benefits along the way can be quite lucrative, and the growth in the value of the business, tax-sheltered.

As a result, the outcomes—tax-assisted wealth creation—can be significant for a family over time. What has been accomplished in this pooling of resources is an expansion of the economic power of the family unit into *the power of a family business unit*—with all the energy of the family focused in one economic direction. In short, many buckets have been assembled to fill the reservoir, as opposed to only one.

There are many fiscal leveraging opportunities. The first dollar of revenue received is used to fund the business activities and lifestyle of the owners and employees; corporate taxes are paid on the remaining net profits. Once again, you have "changed the game" to take control of the ball—your money—but this time with the power of the family's productivity behind you.

There are many tax deferral opportunities as well. Your ability to manage those first dollars in will enable you to increase cash flow available for the activities of business and investing. But even your net dollars available will be bigger, because your corporation pays much lower taxes that you do personally.

For example, retained earnings of the business can be left in the company to invest in the building of the enterprise, or distributed to family shareholders as dividends, at a time that is convenient to the business and tax-efficient to the individual. These dividends are not subject to withholding taxes. They are also tax-preferred on the personal tax return and will, in some cases, actually offset other taxes paid during the year. Often enough dividends can be generated to fund basic lifestyle, *without paying any personal tax at all*.

There's more good news: should the family business be sold, it is possible for family members who are shareholders to each receive up to $750,000 in tax-free gains on their shares. This Capital Gains Deduction is a lucrative reward for the "sweat equity" and financial risks taken by the owners. But in addition, this exemption from tax on the eventual sale of your business can be multiplied when grandchildren arrive, through the use of a family trust. This is very powerful.

That is not to say there aren't several layers of taxes to be paid along the way—personal, corporate, sales, excise taxes and payroll taxes—contributions on the employees' behalf to the Canada Pension Plan (CPP) and Employment Insurance (EI) can all mount up. In fact, there are no shortages of taxing hands in your pocket along the way. However, it is the control over dollars that are more "whole" that can really pay off. Being an employee of your own business puts you in charge of the wealth.

There are lots of reasons to Master Your Taxes as you master your multi-faceted career moves, not the least of which is your increased risks—including the risk of audit as a self-employed person. This is best done in partnership with a tax advisor you can count on to provide "need to know" information so you can make better financial decisions for your time and money. Consider the following as you work on your personal career and the after-tax compensation on your personal return:

1. The difference between employment and self-employment status
2. What's deductible?
3. How to structure family compensation
4. How to win on business equity

THE DIFFERENCE BETWEEN EMPLOYMENT AND SELF-EMPLOYMENT

A business can be a profession, trade or calling of any kind; but it is not an "office or employment", which is specific to the status of an employee. An employee is in a "master-servant relationship" in which reporting of gross earnings and the conditions of employment are left to the employer.

The reporting of income from a business or property, however, starts with the concept of "profit", that is, business owners are taxed on what is left after revenues are reduced by reasonable expenses of creating them. Sometimes, those expenses exceed revenues, in which case, the unincorporated business owner has opportunity to recover some of the deficit on his or her tax return, by offsetting other income of the year. This will reduce the taxes payable. When losses occur in a corporation, they can be used to offset corporate income in prior or future years as well.

This loss deductibility will not be allowed if the activity is a hobby or when expenditures are unreasonable. The key issues that need to be addressed are:

- **Is there a reasonable expectation of profit?** If not, your activities may be a good hobby that may break even, but not a commercial enterprise that will result in profits, and so any loss arising from a hobby will be ignored for income tax purposes. However, any undertaking or activity of a taxpayer that results in profits or has a reasonable prospect of profits would be viewed as the carrying on of a business.

- **When did the business start?** When a personal hobby becomes an organized business activity, may be difficult to determine. To get the best tax advantages, including the determination of an appropriate fiscal year end, it is always helpful to discuss the start of a new business with a professional tax advisor.

- **Are salaries or remuneration paid to family members deductible?** This is also a key question, and will depend upon the terms of engagement of each family member.

There are certainly many "grey areas" when it comes to decisions such as these, and it is therefore not uncommon to see "taxes in dispute". Several years ago the Tax Court of Canada heard an interesting case. At issue was whether the supplier of services to the business was an employee or self-employed as an independent contractor. That difference can provide guidance as to whether statutory deductions required at source—Canada Pension Plan (CPP), Employment Insurance (EI) and Income Taxes— and how income is reported; that is, on a T4 Slip prepared by the employer or, in the case of a subcontract, on an income and expense statement prepared by the contractor.

Four key factors in distinguishing whether a contract *of* service (employment) or a contract *for* service (self-employment) came out of that case:

- Who has control over the work and supervises it
- Who has ownership of tools and income-producing assets
- Amount of financial risk taken for the resulting profits
- The degree of loyalty, continuity or integration the worker has in the enterprise

Employees have very little discretion in the determination of their income, which includes salaries, wages, benefits and other remuneration, including gratuities, received in the calendar year by virtue of employment, and even less over the distribution of after-tax profits of the business, unless they are also shareholders.

Employees have very limited opportunities to claim deductions against their income, as we learned in a prior chapter and must always have the employer sign a declaration of employment conditions that verifies any out-of-pocket expenses claimed were required under the contract of employment. Special rules apply in certain instances, for example:

- **Claiming assets:** Employees cannot generally deduct the cost of acquiring assets like computers. This is often a surprise to many employed commissioned sales people in particular. There are three exceptions to these rules: employees can claim costs associated with motor vehicles, aircraft and musical instruments used in employment. In addition, tradespersons and apprentice vehicle mechanics may be able to deduct a portion of the cost of their tools, and the cost of a power saw used in logging may also be claimed. Very detailed rules govern both the taxation of employer-provided vehicles, allowances paid by the employer for the use of an employee-owned vehicle and the deduction of related expenses.

- **Special occupation-related deductions:** Several occupations can be subject to special rules relating the tools of the trade. For example, while the vast majority of artists are self-employed, employed artists are permitted limited deductions for costs incurred in creating art or in presenting an artistic production. This includes the cost of ballet shoes, body suits, art supplies, computer supplies, home office costs to a maximum of the lesser of 20% of net income or $1,000. Musicians may claim expenses incurred for maintenance, rental, insurance and capital costs of their instruments up to the amount of their income from employment. Certain skilled tradespersons may also claim limited deductions for the cost of their tools.

- **Commissioned sales people:** By virtue of the regulatory requirements imposed upon the negotiation of contracts on behalf of others, licensed commissioned sales people are often considered to be employees, even though they operate in much the same way as a self-employed person, including bearing much of the risk for loss. These folks are provided more flexibility in deducting expenses that relate to the earning their commissions and in some specific cases expenses incurred may exceed commissions earned to offset other income of the year.

It is important for commissioned sales people to clearly understand whether they are considered to be employed or self-employed, to avoid making decisions to commit to expenditures that may not be deductible. The self-employed, as we will discuss below, have much more leeway, as they are considered to be responsible for supervising and controlling work and its outcomes, acquiring assets and bearing the risk of loss. They also have control over the hiring and termination of employees. And they can write off much more of the costs of driving that activity.

The employed/self-employed question comes up often in an audit. Generally the issue is whether source deductions should be taken periodically throughout the year. That's expensive; so is pre-remitting taxes on employment income. The subcontractor certainly has more control over the use of the gross revenues earned—using those resources first in the enterprise or other investments before paying taxes either quarterly or at the end of the year when filing the return.

Business owners may hire family members as employees or subcontractors. However, to be deductible, the work must actually be done, the compensation must be fair and reasonable and the business must otherwise have required the assistance of a stranger to whom the same compensation would have been paid. The subcontractor will also need to prove that he or she has revenue streams from several businesses, rather than only one to cement the position that there is no master-servant relationship.

WHAT'S DEDUCTIBLE?

The key question a new business owner generally has for a tax practitioner is this: "What's deductible?"[1] It would be impossible, no doubt, for the Income Tax Act to list the infinite number of potentially eligible expenditures made to earn income from a commercial enterprise. Instead, the Act provides guidance: the expenditures must be reasonable, have an income-producing purpose and not be personal in nature.

You need to know these parameters to manage decisions about your expenditures, which are broadly classified into four groups—fully deductible, restricted, partially deductible and non-deductible:

Fully deductible expenses are those which are used up in the business: salary, wages, rent, supplies, communication costs, etc.

Restricted expenses include the costs of meals and entertainment; generally, only 50% of these are deductible, although there are some exceptions when all company employees are required to attend certain functions. In that case 100% of the expenditures for meals and entertainment are allowed.

---

[1] In fact, you may be interested in obtaining *Make Sure It's Deductible* by Evelyn Jacks to read an entire book on the subject. See www.knowledgebureau.com

In addition, home office expenses are limited to the amount of net income from the business—they may not create or increase a loss. Where there are "excess" expenses, they can be carried forward and applied against business income next year. See "mixed use" expenses below.

Partially deductible expenses include claims for the depreciation of capital assets, interest costs and "mixed use" expenditures.

Maximizing Capital Cost Allowances

Under the Income Tax Act, this deduction is an estimation of the loss in value based on a declining balance method. That is, assets are placed in a specific class, and a specific percentage, prescribed by law, is applied to the cost to come up with the actual deduction allowed. What's important is that the deduction for these purposes is always taken at the taxpayer's option. This allows us to "save" it for a year in which taxable income is higher, to get a better tax benefit.

In addition, in the first year most assets are acquired, there is a 50% rule: only half the normal deduction is allowed. For this reason, new capital assets to be used in the business are often acquired in the second half of the fiscal year. It is a good idea to discuss the opportunities for timing asset purchases and dispositions with your tax advisor well before year end.

Capitalizing Interest Costs

In difficult economic times, it is interesting to note that some options exist regarding interest costs, which are usually fully deductible. Should the business be in a loss position, it is possible to "capitalize" the cost of interest, and claim it much in the same way as we do the cost of depreciating assets. This election allows the taxpayer to have this provision apply to the current and 3 prior tax years, and may be chosen for all or any portion of the amount of interest. A taxpayer may also wish to make this election during the start up phase of a new business to reduce current losses and have the interest added to the future capital cost allowance claims. Here's an example:

The taxpayer purchased a new building for $1,600,000 on which he used $900,000 of borrowed funds with an interest rate of 4.5%. As the taxpayer is not anticipating any net income from the new building for at least 5 years, his accountant has suggested that he make the election to capitalize the interest paid in the first year. What are the tax consequences?

The $40,500 of interest will be treated as an addition to the capital cost of the building and not deductible as an interest expense.

Source: EverGreen Explanatory Notes, published by The Knowledge Bureau.

Mixed Use Expenditures

As you are aware, there is also a general principle that personal expenditures are not deductible. Therefore personal components of expenditures that have a "**mixed use**" must be removed from otherwise deductible amounts. This involves prorating the expenses or dividing them into portions that are deductible and portions that are not, based on a percentage of business use. Common examples of mixed use expenses include automobile expenses and home office costs, discussed below.

Auto Expenses

These commonly claimed expenses can be a headache at tax time, as this claim is often audited and requires the keeping of a log of travel, which includes both personal and business or employment use. Most people have difficulty keeping that log much past Valentine's Day despite their most earnest New Year's resolution! It appears that even the Finance Department recognizes this, as there is some relief expected from the rules, after consultation with industry, starting in 2009.

The logbook now only needs to be maintained for "a sample period of time" instead of the full year to satisfy a tax auditor. I know you're still groaning, but know you are not alone! In a CFIB August 2007 survey, business owners saw the logbook as a most burdensome compliance issue: 7600 emails in one week said that keeping a mileage log all year long was just too difficult.

There are two types of auto expenses that can be claimed for tax purposes: fixed and operating. The fixed expenses are subject to deductibility restrictions if the taxpayer drives a luxury vehicle (also known as a passenger vehicle). Fixed expenses (and their maximum claimable amounts at the time of writing include:

- Capital Cost Allowance (subject to a maximum cost of $30,000 plus taxes)
- Leasing costs (subject to a maximum of $800 a month plus taxes)
- Interest costs (subject to a maximum of $300 a month)

Operating expenses (fully deductible) include the following costs:

- Fuel and oil, maintenance and repairs
- Insurance, licence and registration fees
- Certain cash expenditures like parking and car washes

Keep the auto log and receipts to be audit proof.

Home Office Expenses

To be eligible for a claim on the tax return, one of two tests must be satisfied:

- The first is that the space is the chief place used to conduct the business.
- The second test is that the space is exclusively used in the conduct of the business activities, and the space is used regularly and on a continuous basis for meeting customers or other people associated with the business. Meeting clients can include phone or in-person meetings.

If the home based business meets either of the two tests, certain expenses of maintaining the home (described below) may be deducted from income. Any such deduction may only be taken based on the proportion of the home office area to the total area of the home. The following fraction is used to make this computation:

$$\frac{\text{Square footage of the home workspace}}{\text{Square footage of the entire living area of the home}} \quad \text{x} \quad \begin{array}{c}\text{Total}\\\text{Expenditures}\\\text{Allowed}\end{array} \quad = \quad \begin{array}{c}\text{Deductible}\\\text{Amount}\end{array}$$

So, you need to set aside some space in the home, measure it, and keep all receipts for home expenses including

- utilities (e.g, heat, hydro, electricity, water)
- monthly rent, condo fees, property taxes, insurance, interest on mortgage
- repair and maintenance costs
- Capital cost allowance (CCA) (although this is not recommended as the Principal Residence exemption will be lost on that portion of the home from which this deduction is taken. See next chapter.)

Non-Deductible Expenses

It's not possible to write off the cost of memberships in social or athletic clubs, more than two conventions in a year, escort services (or any other illicit activities), most fines including speeding tickets, certain advertising costs in foreign media, the costs of maintaining a yacht, or "soft costs" of building or renovations including interest, legal and accounting fees, insurance, and property taxes. Talk to your tax advisor before making those expenditures, and be sure to read later chapters on tackling the tax return and avoiding trouble with CRA!

HOW TO STRUCTURE FAMILY COMPENSATION

Business owners have numerous opportunities to diversify their income sources, split income with family members, increase their working capital by reducing or deferring withholding taxes, decrease personal living costs by writing off the business portion of personal expenses, build equity in the goodwill of their business, and take control of their retirement income and their estate.

The more "buckets" of income and capital we can create within a business structure, the wealthier the family will be. Most businesses will begin as unincorporated ventures, and this can make some sense. Here's why:

The Case for the Unincorporated Structure

There are many reasons to incorporate right away, including legal and risk management issues, and of course the tax minimization and deferral opportunities. However, it may make sense from a tax planning point of view to hold off a bit on a start-up.

A new business will have start up costs. Those costs can result in a loss that can be used to offset other personal income of the current year or, if there is an excess loss, income of the three immediately preceding years. This can be quite lucrative if the entrepreneur started the businesses after leaving an office of employment.

Consider Sarah's situation in our opening scenario, for example. The losses she creates with her business start up costs can offset her employment income and any taxable severance received in the year of termination. Then, excess losses not absorbed by that income can offset employment income in any of the preceding three years. The result will be the recovery of some or all of the taxes she paid while and employee, which may in turn pay for at least some of her start up costs. This recovery of personal income taxes would not be possible if the losses are incurred inside a corporation.

Note that Sarah may also have the opportunity to run her business with a partner, perhaps even her husband. Most families share the burden of business starts. A partnership may be an appropriate way to pool resources. For income tax purposes, a partnership is treated as though it were a person but only for the purposes of computing net income. That net income is allocated to the partners, according to their proportional share of profits as per their partnership agreement and added to their incomes from other sources and taxed in the normal manner. A partnership cannot pay a salary to a partner. It can, however, pay and deduct a reasonable salary to a family member of a partner.

In Canada, however, two other types of structures which are subject to tax: corporations and trusts.

The Case for the Family Business Corporation

All opportunities to arrange family business affairs to build real wealth should be discussed at least annually with the financial advisory team. This includes the right time to move from an unincorporated to a corporate structure. A corporation is a separate entity both at law and for income tax purposes. A corporation affords its owners (shareholders) the protection of limited liability and the ability to pay a variety of different types of distributions: salary, dividends and, eventually, some tax-free gains.

Income from a business carried by a corporation is computed at the corporate level and is taxed at that level—the corporation itself pays tax, but at a much lower rate than individuals. This provides the corporation, and the family, with much larger dollars to retain in the corporation for investment purposes. You can keep those retained earnings in the corporation on a tax deferred basis, paying dividends only when convenient and tax-efficient to do so. Net income of a proprietorship, on the other hand, is taxed in the year earned.

However, income that is earned by a corporation is ultimately subject to tax twice: once in the corporation, and again when dividends are distributed to the shareholders to be reported personally, and therefore some planning is necessary to get intended results.

In addition, when "passive assets"—investments of surplus earnings—on the corporate balance sheet become excessive, the entire structure could be "offside" for the purposes of the $750,000 Capital Gains Deduction, described in more detail below.

Therefore the following checklist of questions may assist business owners in a discussion of compensation and investment planning with their financial advisors and help the inter-advisory team of professionals—tax practitioner, lawyer, insurance and investment specialists—to develop a tax-efficient plan that eliminates the tax risk of building and preserving capital:

- **Personal tax credit use planning:** Should a salary or bonus be paid to a family member to use up available personal credits?
- **Top of bracket planning:** Should income be "topped up" to maximize income reported within lower tax brackets on the personal return? What source of income should be used—bonus, salary or dividends?
- **RRSP and RPP planning:** Should "earned income" be generated to contribute to an RRSP and/or to maximize benefits under a company registered pension plan? Which family members need funding under this plan?
- **Planning for taxable and tax-free benefits:** Should the company fund group health benefits, memberships to athletic clubs, provide employees with autos, low-interest loans or fund education for adult children?
- **Bonus planning:** Should we bonus down to the annual small business limit to pay less corporate tax? Will personal taxes be higher? Should dividends be paid instead?
- **Dividend income planning:** Does the corporation have refundable taxes, and should we consider paying a taxable dividend to recover them?
- **Shareholder loan planning:** Does the owner need to supplement cash flow on a tax-free basis by taking a shareholder loan? When does a shareholder debit balance need to be cleared to avoid income inclusion on the personal return? Will an "imputed interest" benefit relating to the loan be reported on the tax return?
- **Insurance planning:** Which family members should own insurance personally, should the corporation own any, and if so, how should the premiums be paid?

The Case for Trusts

Some families build additional "buckets" for creating and sustaining wealth with a variety of trusts. A trust is not a separate entity at law but a relationship between the settlor of the trust, the trustees and the beneficiaries. For income tax purposes, a trust is a taxpayer and is generally taxed as though it were an individual. One important difference is that a trust cannot claim personal credits.

Another problem is that a trust established during the life of the settlor does not get the benefit of graduated tax rates but pays tax at the top rate applicable to individuals. Testamentary trusts, on the other hand will benefit from graduated rates. These are created on the death of a tax-payer. Trusts are not generally used to carry on a business, although they can be. Trusts can also protect assets from marital property challenges.

A trust is allowed a deduction for income paid or payable to the benefi-ciaries, so that the trustees can generally choose whether tax is to be imposed at the trust level or if the income is to be reported by and taxed in the hands of the beneficiaries. That provides some interesting oppor-tunities for tax planning.

Income flowed through the trust maintains its character—dividends received and allocated are dividends paid to the beneficiaries each year; capital gains are flowed through as capital gains, and so on. In addition, more beneficiaries can be added to the trust as families expand to the third generation.

HOW TO WIN ON BUSINESS EQUITY

When an owner-manager sells a business, the resulting gain on the value of the shares may result in a capital gain, 50% of which is included in income. If the corporation was a qualifying farm, fishing enterprise or small business corporation, that gain could be sheltered by the $750,000 Capital Gains Deduction.

To qualify, the shares must meet these criteria:

- They must be shares of a small business corporation that were not owned by anyone other than the taxpayer, the taxpayer's spouse or common-law partner, or a partnership related to the taxpayer, during the 24-month period before the corporation is sold or disposed of,

- At the time of the disposition, 90% or more of the assets (on a fair market value basis) must be used principally (more than 50%) in an active business carried on primarily (also more than 50%) in Canada,

- During the 24-month period prior to the disposition, the corporation's assets (on a fair market value basis) were used primarily (more than 50%) in an active business carried on primarily in Canada,

- During the 24-month period prior to disposition, the shares were shares in a Canadian controlled private corporation.

What this means is that if four adult shareholders in a family sold their family business for a gain of $3,000,000, none of that gain would be subject to tax! Now that's real wealth management! But there is more good news.

One of the most lucrative benefits that can flow from the use of a family trust is that it can multiply access to the $750,000 Capital Gains Deduction. This can be done because a trust can allocate a capital gain to the beneficiaries and, should the gain have arisen on the disposition of qualified property, each of the beneficiaries can claim his or her Capital Gains Deduction against the gain. Therefore, astute business owners will want to discuss the following with their advisors:

- **Capital Gains Deduction planning:** Make sure assets within your operating company meet the 50% or 90% test—too many "passive" investments in the operating company's accounts could compromise accessibility to the Capital Gains Deduction.

- **Surplus fund planning:** When should surplus funds be paid out to the shareholders to invest personally, rather remaining in the corporation?

IN SUMMARY

If you are unsure about how these structures may fit with your wealth accumulation goals, consider an educational session with your tax accountant, financial and legal advisor. This will pay off. It is also important to have a family vision for exit strategies, particularly if adult children work in the business, and a format around which a family counsel can be structured to discuss these important matters. This type of formal communication will help the family to preserve wealth and transition it successfully down the line, when mom and dad need a retirement income, and children need the authority to operate the business.

So it's not a bad idea to initiate this formal family chat annually; possibly around the issues of strategic philanthropy as a family goal for leadership training.

THINGS YOU NEED TO KNOW

- There are tax advantages to being both employed and self-employed.
- Start up losses in a proprietorship may help you recover taxes paid during employment stints.
- Properly structured, each adult family member could earn a $750,000 tax-free capital gain on the sale or disposition of a qualifying small business corporation.
- Your relationship with the tax department will change significantly as a self-employed person and your likelihood of audit will increase.
- However, you will have control of the first dollar you earn and a more significant role in the creation of significant family wealth as a result of numerous options for compensation structures and income tax deferral.

QUESTIONS YOU NEED TO ASK

- Should I be employed or self-employed or both?
- What are the tax advantages of owning a small business?
- Does mine have a reasonable expectation of profit?
- How do I plan my tax-efficient compensation?
- Are salaries or remuneration paid to family members deductible?
- How can I cash in on the Capital Gains Deduction?

THINGS YOU NEED TO DO

- Discuss the various "buckets" of income and investment you can create to maximize your wealth creation opportunities.
- Understand how to manage your risk by reviewing your insurance policies: disability and death.
- Find out how your relationship with CRA will change once you are self-employed.
- Plan with the end in mind: your retirement income plan and your wealth transition plan by setting up a family council.
- Work with the right financial advisory team, selecting one most trusted advisor to help you make financial decisions that are powerful.

Principle Mastery: When you understand your personal economic power, and then multiply it to include family resources of horsepower and capital, you will preside over powerful family wealth creation opportunities. However, the right tax-efficient structures must be put in place to better secure your future. It therefore pays to Master Your Taxes relating to your options early in your career.

MASTER YOUR TAXES
Masterful Career Moves

TIPS

- You may be a powerful earner as an employee and that's an important way to cut your teeth, gain experience, build relationships and shore up wealth that could later be used in a business start up.

- You could have more control over your family's wealth by structuring different compensation models by starting a business within a corporate or trust setting.

- The opportunity to earn tax-free wealth—by selling shares in a small business corporation for example—is a lucrative opportunity.

- The ability to control and diversify your compensation, through salary, dividends, taxable and tax-free benefits and income splitting, can significantly increase your wealth over the long run.

- Risk comes in all forms—risk of unemployment, risk of bankruptcy, risk of audit, risk of marketplace volatility, risk of illness and death.

- Risk can be diversified away however, with your ability to use your talents and resources in the most effective way, and this can include self-employment.

- Explore those opportunities with a competent professional team who knows and understands your vision, mission and goals.

TRAPS

- Business ownership is not for everyone.

- According to a recent survey by the CFIB[2], by the year 2013, 41% of business owners in Canada are expected to exit their businesses, yet over 60% of entrepreneurs age 55 to 64 have yet to discuss their plans with their families. This is both an opportunity for successors and a recipe for failure for family business transition in Canada.

- Failure to keep your eye on your relationship with CRA can result in audit risk.

---

[2] Canadian Federation of Independent Business Survey, Report on Succession, 2004

CHAPTER 5

Finances:
Your Tax-Free Nest

It's kind of fun to do the impossible. WALT DISNEY

Thomas was delighted to graduate with his business degree and immediately find himself placed in a junior executive position with a large marketing firm; something he could only have dreamed of five years ago when he started university. A smart man, 24-year old Thomas lived at home throughout university, saved his money from jobs he held while studying, and found himself debt-free and ready to invest. His parents gifted him a significant sum towards a down payment on a home. He was unsure about committing to something so long term...real estate was really quite scary for Thomas...there were so many decisions to make.

- *Is an investment in a principal residence really the right thing to do at such a young age?*
- *Should he invest in the stock market or save toward his retirement instead?*
- *Are there any tax advantages doing one over the other?*
- *How much debt should he take on?*
- *How will his own home purchase affect the potential inheritance of his parent's home when they retire to the cottage over the next two years?*

THE ISSUES

Ownership of a principal residence is a cornerstone of wealth for Canadians. Statistics Canada[1] has reported that 60% of all Canadians own their own homes. Better yet, half of those homeowners have paid off their mortgage. Despite fluctuations in the marketplace, the trend to secure homeownership in Canada has contributed to the increased wealth of boomers and their parents today; relative to their ancestors of the 1950s.

One of the reasons why home ownership is so attractive to Canadians is that the increase in value of a property designated as a principal residence is never taxed—neither are the actual capital gains that may be received on the sale or transfer of the home. A tax exempt asset is the best kind, by far!

It's easy to qualify too. A principal residence could be a house, a cottage, a mobile home, a condo, or a recreation property like a condo in Florida, a cottage on the Lake of the Woods, or a ski chalet in Whistler. All Thomas needs to do is to live in the property at some time in every year in which it is declared to be his "principal residence". Is there a particular length of stay required? The answer is no. The Income Tax Act simply requires that you "ordinarily inhabit the property at some time during the year". That can mean a weekend, two weeks, two months—it's up to you.

The issues for any homeowner really revolve around understanding how to maximize tax exemptions for their personal residences, how to fund the purchase of the property, and how to transfer personal residences amongst family members most advantageously. The tax system has made this relatively easy for most, as home ownership is encouraged through a variety of tax advantaged savings plans.

THE SOLUTIONS

In our true-to-life scenario, Thomas could buy a home, live in it for a couple of months, wait for its value to rise by a significant amount, then sell it and not pay a dime of tax! That's because in Canada one personal residence per household may qualify for tax exempt status as the principal residence, in each year that it is owned and "ordinarily inhabited".

---

[1] The Wealth of Canadians, May 2007, Statistics Canada

In fact, in this case, Thomas wouldn't even have to declare the sale of his home on the tax return—unless he owned another personal residence at the same time. In that case, he would simply choose one of the properties to be his "tax exempt principal residence." This is done on a year over year basis, so it is possible for the two properties to have "exempt" status at different times in the ownership period.

More about how to do those calculations later.

What's important in either scenario is that Thomas must meet the inhabitation test and actually live in each property *at some time during the year*. The Income Tax Act is not specific about how long.

A principal residence is a strong catalyst in accumulating wealth, despite the fact that most taxpayers go into significant debt to fund it, and interest paid on a mortgage for the principal residence is not tax deductible. However, depending on how strategic Thomas is about his investments, he could eventually leverage the equity from his personal residence to create more wealth. That is, when there is equity in a personal residence, homeowners can obtain investment loans and use that equity as security. Resulting interest payments on the investment loan are now tax deductible if there is the potential to earn income from the newly acquired investments.

So, if Thomas can afford to pay down a mortgage, he should invest in a tax exempt principal residence. Fortunately, Thomas has many options for a Principal Residence Mastery Plan. Consider the following solutions:

- The Family Income Splitting Plan
- The Roommate Assistance Plan
- The RESP Solution
- The Tax-Free Savings Account
- The RRSP Tax Savings Plan
- The RRSP Home Buyers' Plan
- The Accelerated Mortgage Retirement Plan
- The Employer-Funded Taxable Benefit Plan
- The Quick Flip Plan

The Family Income Splitting Plan

One of the best ways Thomas' parents could set up his financial future is to gift him the money for a down payment on a home used as a principal residence. Resulting capital gains on the sale of the property will not be attributed back to his parents. That means the parents won't have a tax consequence for the gains this gifted money results in. Those gains, in fact, are tax exempt. Therefore, it makes sense for parents of adult children to consider moving some of their own surplus savings into a tax exempt principal residence for their adult children. There are some tax-efficient ways to think about in coming up with the cash flow to do so.

- **Distribute dividends from a family business to the adult child,** to be used for the purpose of funding the home purchase. In many provinces the amount of dividends receivable before paying tax is significant. Check out the Marginal Tax Rates at the back of this book on dividend income and ask your tax accountant to help you plan dividend income for the adult child to fund a down payment or ongoing payments.

- **At tax time, identify tax savings from tuition, education, and textbook credits and transfers** (and in some provinces graduate tax credits); then deposit those extra tax savings to the savings account used for the purpose of saving for the home or paying down the mortgage.

The Roommate Assistance Plan

That principal residence for college-bound sons and daughters can help defray expensive apartment rental costs while building tax exempt equity in the home itself. If your child, like Thomas, is mature enough to keep the property up to maintain and enhance its value, you may be able to supplement the costs of the property with rentals to other university-bound friends. Your child would live rent free. This would cut down non-deductible personal living costs during the university days and may fund food and clothing expenses along the way. The principal residence exemption on this property will not, incidentally, be compromised by the occasional rental income *as long as Capital Cost Allowance (CCA) is not claimed as a deduction on the building.*[2]

---

[2] Capital Cost Allowance is a notional deduction which accounts for depreciation on the building on what's known in accounting terms as a declining balance basis. Be sure to ask your tax advisor about this.

The Registered Education Savings Plan (RESP) Solution

Most people know that an RESP is a tax-assisted savings plan set up for the purpose of funding a beneficiary's future education costs. It also serves as a way to split income earned in the plan with the beneficiary, who will normally be taxed at a lower rate than the contributor when earnings are withdrawn.

So what's the connection to home ownership? There are no restrictions for the use of the RESP funds other than the student, who must be at least age 16, is enrolled in a qualifying educational program. The payments from the RESP, called the Education Assistance Payments (EAPs), can be used to fund the student's living costs including costs associated with home ownership. That's a good way for a student to leverage tax deferred savings and pay those costs of owning a home.

The Tax-Free Savings Account

The TFSA is a powerful new savings plan for individuals who deposit money into this account starting in January 2009. Every year each individual in the family who is at least age 18 is gifted $5000[3] of "unused TFSA Room", just by filing a tax return. Unlike an RRSP deposit, no deduction is allowed when the money is contributed to the TFSA. That means you fund it with "tax paid" dollars. However, withdrawals from the plan of both capital and investment earnings are tax-free. Plus, as an added bonus, those withdrawals create an equivalent amount of unused TFSA contribution room for future tax-free savings.

Imagine the power of leaving your money in a savings account that earns income from property—interest, dividends or capital gains, for example—never to be taxed while it is in the TFSA account—nor when you take it out. The full amount of your investment earnings on your deposit are added to the capital balance again and again, growing, tax-free within the plan.

Even better, you can then withdraw these savings on a completely tax-free basis and use them for any purpose, including home ownership.

---

[3] Indexing of this $5000 amount will be applied in increments of $500, which means the $5000 limit will rise in line with an adjustment for inflation.

There is absolutely no tax on your earnings and no restrictions on the use of the money. You don't even lose the TFSA contribution room that is left by your withdrawal. You can, in fact, recontribute amounts withdrawn to the TFSA, to build up your tax-free savings once again.

The TFSA is a great investment for managing shorter term savings goals like money for home improvements. Here's an example:

> At the age of 18, Thomas is gifted $5000 to open a TFSA account by his parents. He then saves $5000 in each of the next 5 years in the TFSA, achieving capital contributions of $30,000. During that six year period, his average return on the investment was 3%, leaving him with accumulated capital and earnings of $32,824. That's $323 more than if he had saved the money outside of the TFSA, because the earnings in the TFSA were not taxed.

> If he earned a 5% return on his TFSA, his accumulated capital would grow to $34,849—$2025 more than under the 3% scenario and $569 more than if he saved the same capital outside the TFSA. That's a significant down payment for a starter home in only 6 years.

> Assume that Thomas withdraws this amount and invests it in his home, leaving unused TFSA contribution room of an equivalent amount. Essentially he can re-invest the amount he put into the TFSA, without being restricted to a $5000 yearly limit. His plan is to fill that TFSA gap with tax savings gleaned from his RRSP contributions over the next several years. Then he can withdraw funds from his TFSA again, tax-free, for home improvements he wishes to make.

The RRSP Tax Savings Plan

Many people are not aware that RRSPs can be a route to home ownership as well as retirement savings. But the plan is not seamless: certain criteria must be met.

While there is no lower age limit for contributing to a Registered Retirement Savings Plan, there are two other restrictions: first, the contributor must have "earned income" at least in a preceding year to build "RRSP Contribution Room". This earned income will come largely from active income sources like employment or self-employment. RRSP contribution room that is not used in one year can be carried forward. However, be mindful of the second restriction: the contributor to an RRSP cannot be older than 71.

Most students live on a shoestring. In Thomas' case, assuming he has qualifying earned income and therefore unused RRSP contribution room, an RRSP contribution, which his parents might make for him, can be used to generate some much needed cash.

First, it will result in a tax deduction and tax savings based on Thomas' marginal tax rate. Let's assume that's 30%, as he is a working student. Therefore, an annual contribution of $5000 to an RRSP will reap tax savings of $1500.

Thomas' plan is to invest those tax savings back into his TFSA account every year until he finishes university five years from now, to build up a home maintenance and improvement fund. After the 5 years, at a rate of return of 5%, he will have just under $8500 in savings: enough for a new deck, a new driveway, or a hot tub for the back yard. That's good tax planning.

Because he has accumulations in his RRSP, Thomas has yet another tax advantaged option in his home ownership planning, should he need more money, to build a deck, for example.

The RRSP Home Buyers' Plan

Taxpayers who save money within an RRSP usually do so to fund their retirement. In those cases, withdrawals of any kind from the RRSP (principal and earnings) will be added to income in the year of withdrawal. However, it is possible to withdraw money from the RRSP on a tax-free basis for two other purposes: the purchase of a residence and the funding of a return to school.

The Home Buyers' Plan allows first time home buyers (or those who have not owned a home in the current year or preceding four years) to withdraw up to $20,000 from their RRSP on a tax-free basis, for the purpose of buying or building a home. No tax will be withheld on such withdrawals. The withdrawals may be a single amount or the taxpayer may make a series of withdrawals throughout the year as long as the total does not exceed $20,000. Application for withdrawal of RRSP amounts is made on Form T1036 *Home Buyers' Plan (HBP) Request to Withdraw Funds from an RRSP.*

Tax-free withdrawals from an RRSP may also be made for the purpose of making home renovations to meet the needs of a disabled person. It is not necessary that the taxpayer actually use the funds borrowed for the intended purpose, only that they buy or build the qualifying home. Yes, that means you can buy furniture and a vacation too.

But there is one catch: The funds used under the Home Buyers' Plan must be repaid back into the RRSP, over a period not exceeding 15 years, beginning in the second calendar year after the withdrawal. There's a tax consequence if you don't: amounts which are due and not repaid must be included in the taxpayer's income in the year they are due. So, that may make withdrawing money from the RRSP a less tax-efficient vehicle than the TFSA for the purposes of home ownership.

The Accelerated Mortgage Retirement Plan

Mortgage interest on a personal residence is not tax deductible. Therefore it makes sense to retire the mortgage as quickly as possible. One way to do that is to make lump sum payments annually to reduce your mortgage balance. Yet another strategy is to reduce your amortization period (10 years instead of 25 for example) and your interest rate (5% instead of 6%). The following example follows a $150,000 mortgage with monthly payments and an interest rate set at 6%:

A. **Terms: 25 year amortization:** $960/mo payments, total interest paid $137,913

B. **10 year amortization:** $1,660/mo payments, total interest $49,172; **Savings are $88,741!**

C. **Interest rate reduced to 5%,** 25 year amortization: $872/mo payments, total interest $111,721; **Savings are $26,192!**

Source: CanadaMortgage.com.

Imagine, you could fund the purchase of another property by paying your mortgage down quickly! These powerful strategies will help you reduce non-deductible debt, especially if you are concerned about a credit crunch. You can then remortgage your home for business or investment purposes if you like, and write off the interest on those loans, too.

The Employer-Funded Taxable Benefit Plan

Sometimes employees are lucky enough to negotiate a low interest loan from their employer. The benefit of receiving this loan may be taxable. This will show up on the T4 slip. If the loan was used for investment purposes, this taxable benefit can be written off as an investment carrying charge.

These benefits can be extended to family members who are employees of the family business or shareholders of the business, provided that these are bona fide loan arrangements, repaid over a reasonable period of time. It must be shown that the loan is a direct result of the employer-employee relationship rather than the shareholder relationship. (This means that the company must make such loans available to all employees.)

Parents of children who work in the family business may well offer a low interest loan, to be used to fund the purchase of a tax exempt principal residence. This is a good way to use corporate dollars, which are taxed at lower rates, to enhance the lifestyle of the family member and help to build tax exempt wealth for your children too.

This is also a great example of "paying yourself first". In this case, you are using your employer's tax paid dollars and paying tax on the taxable benefit later.

The Quick Flip Plan

The Income Tax Act puts no limit on the number of tax exempt principal residences one can own in a lifetime. Thomas can buy a home, fix it up, sell it for a tax exempt profit and then do it again and again. Many taxpayers build significant tax exempt wealth in this way.

However, one needs to be careful. There are a couple of provisions that could leave you with unintended results: a fully taxable gain rather than a tax exempt gain:

1. **The Designation of Principal Residence.** You can only designate one property as your principal residence in any year. A special "1+ provision" effectively allows 2 per year, but that's the limit. These rules are discussed in more detail below.

2. **Are these activities an "adventure or concern in the nature of trade"?** In other words, is this a business activity? The *Income Tax Act* does not prescribe when gains from the sale of real estate will be considered to be income rather than capital or exempt. Generally, when the intention of the taxpayer is to earn income from the sale of real estate, the income will be included in income from business and is taxable. In making such determinations, the courts have considered factors such as:

    - the taxpayer's intention at the time of the purchase: residence or investment?
    - geographical location and zoned use of the real estate acquired
    - the terms of the financing
    - the length of time the property was held by the taxpayer
    - factors which motivated the sale of the real estate, and
    - evidence that the taxpayer had dealt extensively in real estate transactions

3. **Is this a business property?** When the property is held for its use in a business and its value increases, the gain on sale is considered to be "capital" in nature, and could be subject to a 50% income inclusion. You may use a principal residence as a home based business without worrying about losing the exempt status, but as mentioned earlier, you must be sure not to claim Capital Cost Allowance.

4. **Is the buying and selling of the homes part of your occupation?**
   The more closely a taxpayer's business or occupation (e.g. a builder, a real estate agent) is related to any real estate transactions, the more likely it is that any gains realized by the taxpayer from the sale of his properties will be considered to be business income (fully taxable) rather than a capital gain or exempt gain.

MORE THAN ONE RESIDENCE

Your tax-free nest may well be affected by ownership in other residences. If you do own more than one personal residence, the good news is that you can choose which one should be the exempt residence, provided you met the inhabitation rules—that is you must have "ordinarily inhabited" each property to choose it as a tax exempt principal residence.

You would of course choose the home that appreciated the most in value as the tax exempt one. Trouble is, you may sell the properties at different times. Here's what you need to know and discuss with your tax advisor:

Residences owned prior to 1982

It has only been since 1972 that gains on the increase in the value of assets have been taxable. And, in the ten year period leading to December 31, 1981, each spouse in the family could own one tax exempt principal residence. In those days, it was not unusual for families to own two properties: one in the city and one at the lake or in the mountains, and then reap the rewards of a tax exempt gain on each property sold in the period.

Where more than one property is owned, and the family uses both at some time during the year, the calculation of the tax exempt capital gain is more difficult. For any gains accrued in the period including 1971 to 1981, the principal residence tax exempt will shelter both properties.

For ownership periods starting in 1982, when only one property per year can be designated as a principal residence for the family, accrued capital gains on one of the properties will be ultimately subject to tax when sold. It is important to have a valuation of the property as of December 31,

1981 to assist with your calculations on a form CRA has devised for those purposes, described below.

Other significant valuation dates for principal residences include the following:

- Pre 1972: no tax on accrued gains on any capital assets
- 1972 to 1981: one principal residence designation allowed for each year for each spouse
- 1982 to date: one principal residence allowed for each year to each family unit in which there was legal married status
- 1993 to date: one principal residence designation allowed for each year to each conjugal relationship (married or common-law)
- 2001 to date: same-sex couples required to limit themselves to one principal residence designation per year per conjugal relationship

When these households own more than one personal residence, they must choose one property as the tax exempt property and one as the taxable property.

Form T2091 *Designation of a Property as a Principal Residence by an Individual (Other Than a Personal Trust)* is used to calculate the exempt portion of a capital gain on a principal residence, in cases where there is a taxable portion. You will be asked to tell your tax advisor the number of years each property you own is to be designated as a principal residence, so that you can calculate the "exempt" portion. It is not necessary to designate the year of sale or transfer, as the computations will add a "grace year" to the formula.

Always get a valuation of all principal residences owned when any of them are sold or transferred so that you can make the right choices on your principal residence designation form. *Also be aware that by not reporting the sale of a personal residence you are implicitly designating it as your principal residence for all years that you owned it.*

Also, keep all receipts for any repairs to all the homes; if any of them are taxable, you'll be able to reduce your tax bill by adding your additional expenditures to the original cost base. You'll learn more about calculating capital gains in a later chapter.

Finally, the cost base of your personal residence may be affected by any Capital Gains Election made on February 22, 1994, the day on which the $100,000 Capital Gains Deduction was eliminated. We'll discuss this in more detail later in the book, but for now know this is a form (T664) you should look for before recording a disposition.

Change in Use of Principal Residence

When a taxpayer starts using a principal residence for income-producing purposes (rental, home office) there are a number of important consequences to consider:

- You must get the property appraised when there is a change of use, as the property is considered to be disposed of at its Fair Market Value (FMV) and then immediately reacquired at the same amount. The gain resulting, if any, would be nil if the home was used in each year before this as a principal residence. However, you may have an immediate tax consequence if you owned another residence that perhaps has appreciated in value more, thereby being your preferred choice for the principal residence exemption.

- If the property is converted back to be used as a principal residence only, there is another deemed disposition and reacquisition of the property to account for. Tax consequences could result.

The good news is that in these cases an election may be made to ignore the deemed dispositions for now and defer any capital gain/loss until the time of actual sale or transfer sometime in the future. In the case of a sale, at least you'll have the money to pay the taxes then. Check this out with your tax advisor and real estate appraiser before you change the use of your property. Deemed dispositions of property are discussed in a later chapter.

Rental Property Becomes Principal Residence

It is also possible to make a special election which notifies CRA of your wish to defer taxes when a taxpayer converts a rental property to a principal residence. In that case, there is a deemed disposition at FMV, but the capital gain is deferred to be reported on the actual disposition of the property. *This is only allowed, however, if no capital cost allowance was claimed on the property.*

Use of Principal Residence for Business Purposes

If you use a part of your home for income-producing purposes, (for example child care in the home, boarders in the home or office-in-the-home) your tax exemption will not be affected if you set aside a specific area for the income-producing activity and again do not claim Capital Cost Allowance on the building. Home business expenses were discussed in an earlier chapter.

Employer-Required Moves

There is an important exception to the "inhabitation" rules you should know about if you are a mobile employee. If your employer requires you to relocate to another city, you may not be able sell your home, or perhaps may want to keep it (choosing to rent in the work location instead). In such a case you can also choose to designate your home as a tax exempt principal residence even though you have not technically inhabited it.

This is possible for up to four years after moving out of the house[4]. You could even choose to rent out your home in the meantime, and then move back into it without losing your principal residence exemption; however you may not designate a different property as your principal residence during this time. You must move back into the home before the end of the calendar year in which your employment is terminated and, of course, you must report the rental income and expenses. Check with your tax advisor about the elections you must file in this case.

---

[4] Longer if the new work location is at least 40 kilometres away

IN SUMMARY

Your principal residence may well be the most significant asset you own and one that will contribute substantially to your family wealth because its value accrues on a tax-free and tax exempt basis. The sooner an adult family member can invest in a principal residence, the faster he or she is on their way to maximizing a tax exempt asset.

THINGS YOU NEED TO KNOW

- A principal residence can be a completely tax exempt asset.
- To elect a property to be your principal residence, you have to have inhabited it at some time in the year.
- There are many tax-efficient ways young people can save for a home on a tax-preferred basis.
- Accelerating the retirement of your mortgage is wise, as interest is not deductible.
- Sometimes, family members who are employed by a family business can use corporate dollars to fund home purchases.
- Up to two tax exempt principal residences can be owned in one year or several throughout your lifetime; however too many quick flips might put you in the real estate "business".
- When two or more properties are owned, it may be necessary to calculate the exempt portion of a gain on sale, if one property was previously used as the exempt one.
- When you change the use of your personal residence, it is a taxable event. You need to get a fair market evaluation, but can usually elect to defer paying taxes until there is an actual sale.
- You can move out of your principal residence for up to four years, rent it out, move back in and still not disqualify yourself from using the principal residence exemption, if your employer required you to move away to work.

QUESTIONS YOU NEED TO ASK

- Can I afford to buy a principal residence?
- How will I fund it, and its maintenance?
- How can I pay the least interest over time on my mortgage?
- How can I leverage my home equity?
- How can I maximize my principal residence exemption if I end up owning more than one property?
- What are the tax consequences of moving from my city home to my country home upon my retirement?
- Should I put the cottage in a family trust to preserve it for the future?

THINGS YOU NEED TO DO

- Save as much money as possible in a TFSA, RRSP, RESP, and non-registered accounts.
- Buy a house you can afford. Pay down the mortgage quickly to save money on interest costs and preserve your wealth for other investments.
- Consider the benefits of using some of the equity in your home to back loans to make other investments.
- Try to find low interest loans to make these investments—your employer may be a good source.
- Keep receipts for all repairs and maintenance made to your homes. They could be used to reduce future capital gains.
- Get valuations of properties when there is a change of use and on significant valuation dates: December 31, 1971 and December 31, 1981.
- Existing property owners should be sure to dig out Form T664 Capital Gains Election. This form was used to make an election to bump the cost base of assets owned on February 22, 1994—the day the $100,000 Capital Gains Deduction was eliminated. The information is important for executors too. Without it, you'll overpay tax on the disposition of elected assets.

DECISIONS YOU NEED TO MAKE

- Do I want to commit to an investment in home ownership?
- How do I fund the home?
- How many personal residences do I want to own and where?

MASTER YOUR TAXES
The Tax-Free Nest: Personal Residences

TIPS

- Home ownership is so attractive to Canadians because accrued gains in value of a principal residence may never be taxed.
- Live in the property at some time in every year to qualify the property as a potential tax exempt principal residence.
- Your condo, trailer, detached home in the city, cottage, villa, farm, or home in Florida could qualify as your principal residence.
- Use deposits from the new TFSA to fund your home purchase.
- Other opportunities exist under the Home Buyers' Plan feature within an RRSP.
- Leverage your tax savings from an RRSP contribution, and build your down payment (or pay down the mortgage) more quickly.
- Get valuations for your properties when there is a change of use
- Don't forget to save receipts for all repairs and improvements to your properties.
- Consult your tax professional to help you sort out the principal residence election where more than one personal residence is owned.
- Employer-required moves can result in tax leniency: principal residence exemptions can be preserved, some losses on the sale of your home can be covered by your employer on a tax exempt basis, home relocation loans may be negotiated at tax-preferred rates. Discuss this with your tax advisor.

TRAPS

- Don't claim Capital Cost Allowance on a home that may be used as a tax exempt principal residence.
- Remember, interest paid on a mortgage for the principal residence is not tax deductible. Pay it off quickly—keep more from the deal.
- Losses on the sale of your personal residences are not deductible.

- Many home owners made a Capital Gains Election on their taxable residences on February 22, 1994 to use up their $100,000 Capital Gains Deduction which was eliminated on that day. Be sure to take this into account in determining the cost based of a property when recording dispositions of personal properties.

Principle Mastery: Your investment in a personal residence for each adult in the family can result in thousands of dollars in tax exempt gains upon each sale or disposition!

CHAPTER 6

Finances:
Tax-Preferred Investment Strategies

*Over and over again courts have said that there is nothing sinister in so
arranging one's affairs as to keep taxes as low as possible. Everybody does so,
rich and poor; and all do right, for nobody owes any public duty to pay more
than the law demands.* JUSTICE LEARNED HAND

> *"Did I really lose 50% in my retirement portfolio?" Don was more
> than concerned. He was incredulous. He had spent a lifetime
> working hard, saving his money, and now, it seemed his future
> was less secure than ever. His half a million dollar portfolio was
> now worth half as much.*
>
> *"Don, we have our health, and so we can continue to work and
> save to make up for the losses." Judy was a realist. She knew that
> there was nothing to do but to carry on. But she was intrigued by
> a conversation she had had with the couple's tax advisor that day.*
>
> *"Did you know, Don, that with a better eye on our tax outcomes,
> we might be able to replace some of those losses through our tax
> refunds this year?*
>
> *Don looked up from his investment statement; he was intrigued
> too. "Well, we certainly should look for all the help we can get…"*

THE ISSUES

How much does it take to re-accumulate $250,000 over the next ten years—the time Don has left until retirement? Simple math would tell you that's $25,000 in new savings every year, and that's a lot of new money—an impossible savings goal for most, unless a lottery or inheritance suddenly falls out of the sky.

Consider going forward Don might earn a 5 % annually compounding return on his investments. He'd be able to recover his portfolio losses in just under 15 years. However he could afford to earn half that amount—2.5%, which may be much more realistic in the short term—if he added new capital of $8791 each year; more possible, but still difficult. Can tax-efficiency help? Absolutely. There are several things Don and Judy can do to create the new capital, tax efficiently now, but then also to ensure their gains are not taxed away later. For example:

- Make RRSP Contributions and invest the tax savings.
- Make TFSA Contributions to ramp up savings for next year, tax-free.
- Reduce tax withholding at source and recalculate quarterly instalments payments due March, June, September and December; then reinvest the savings.
- Increase this year's tax refund: really dig for every tax deduction and credit they are entitled to.
- Split income, possibly by speeding up entitlements to their company-sponsored pension plan.
- Take an early retirement benefit from the Canada Pension Plan, split the income and invest both the benefits and the savings.
- Transfer portfolio winners to their favorite charity: a great way to avoid tax on capital gains and get money back from their charitable donation receipt.
- Carry losses back to offset taxes paid on previously reported capital gains.
- Buy depreciable assets to increase deduction for Capital Cost Allowances.

- Reduce mortgage interest and credit card payments, then invest the savings.
- Take a second job or consulting contract...
- Rent out a room in the house...
- Stop feeding the kids cheese...

SOLUTIONS

Tax-efficient investing is the process of taking advantage of tax rules (often called tax preferences) so as to pay the least amount of taxes on income, and accumulate the most after-tax wealth for the family over a lifetime, and beyond. That implies not just process, but strategy too.

Strategy and process are always important. This helps you get through good times and bad. Your plans will provide selection of investment products, and the structure in which they will grow which can significantly influence the accumulation of family wealth, especially if you plan them with tax-efficiency.

Don and Judy needed to focus on their wealth accumulations again, but this time, with shorter time horizons. They needed to focus on creating the right source of income, at the right time to increase cash flow, so they could save and reinvest more in these difficult times. When you invest with the best tax outcomes in mind, you can recover ground quickly.

Strategic tax-efficient investment income planning will have significant short term benefits but as well significant long term effects on wealth creation, growth, preservation and transition. When you factor in the effect of inflation and costs into the process, you have the process of Real Wealth Management™.

Trouble is, many people don't understand how to integrate a long term tax, inflation and cost-efficient focus into their investment activities. This has quickly been proven as investors have flown out of the stock market to what they consider to be "safe" Guaranteed Investment Certificates (GICs) and other interest-bearing debt obligations.

Most people, for example, know what a Canada Savings Bond is. This common investment vehicle is issued by the federal government. The lender (you, the investor) receives interest in return for the right to the use of your money. What you're hoping for is a guaranteed return of principal and income resulting from the use of your money by government.

Unfortunately that's a false hope. Why? Because, when you take taxes and inflation into account, most investors will actually loose money on their CSB investment because it is not tax-efficient. Interest is subject to a high marginal rate of tax, as demonstrated below:

Real After-tax Return of $1,000 Compounding CSB*

Year	Interest Earned	Taxes	Inflation Adjustment	Principal and Earnings Left**	Real After Tax Return
Principal	$1000.00				
0	Plus:	Less:	Less:		
1	$18.00	($5.58)	($30.00)	$982.42	(1.76%)
2	$18.32	($5.68)	($29.47)	$965.59	(1.71%)
3	$18.65	($5.78)	($28.97)	$949.49	(1.67%)
4	$18.99	($5.89)	($28.48)	$934.11	(1.62%)
5	$19.33	($5.99)	($28.02)	$919.43	(1.57%)
6	$19.68	($6.10)	($27.58)	$905.42	(1.52%)
7	$20.03	($6.21)	($27.16)	$892.08	(1.47%)
8	$20.39	($6.32)	($26.76)	$879.39	(1.42%)
9	$20.76	($6.44)	($26.38)	$867.34	(1.37%)
10	$21.14	($6.55)	($26.02)	$855.90	(1.32%)
Total	**$1195.30**	**($60.54)**	**($278.86)**	**$855.90**	**(14.41%)**

* Assumes 1.8% interest rate, inflation at 3% and a 10-year hold period. Taxpayer is in 31% tax bracket.
** Amount shown in current-year dollars (i.e. adjusted for inflation from year 0).

Is this the best after-tax return for your money? Well, no. Your return after taxes and inflation, after 10 years is actually a loss of 14.41% in real dollar terms. Could another type of investment be more tax-efficient? Possibly. These are the questions that need to be put to your tax and financial advisors.

To keep your eye on "real" returns—after tax, after inflation and after taking into account the costs associated with the investment—the following strategies for tax-efficient investing should be considered, and then link the appropriate investment products to the strategy:

- Avoid tax entirely
- Defer tax on income
- Blend income and capital for tax-preferred cash flow
- Reduce tax using tax preferences and income splitting techniques
- Shift taxes to lower income earners or into alternate tax structures
- Minimize capital withdrawals to pay taxes or instalments.

AVOID TAX ENTIRELY

The best tax strategy is to pay no tax on your investments at all. One way to do this is to keep taxable income levels under the taxpayer's "tax-free zone". Due to the Basic Personal Amount, for most these days that's about $10,000, but it can be more, depending on other available tax deductions and credits during the year.

Another way to pay no tax is to invest in assets that are tax exempt. For example:

1. The new Tax-Free Savings Accounts (TFSA)
2. Certain insurance policy products
3. A tax exempt principal residence (discussed in a prior chapter)

The Tax-Free Savings Account

Because the TFSA is so new, it is important that you understand its potentially powerful position in your portfolio. Available starting January 1, 2009, the new Tax-Free Savings Account (TFSA) is a registered account in which investment earnings, including capital gains accumulate tax-free. Its benefits are as clear as its name: *you earn the income it produces tax-free.*

Investors must be 18 to contribute up to $5,000 each year to such an account and they must have "TFSA contribution room" to do so, which is created by simply filing a tax return. The maximum deposit level will be indexed and adjusted in $500 increments in the future. There is no upper age barrier, which means you can contribute annually for the rest of your life.

If a taxpayer's TFSA contribution room is not used in one year it may be carried forward to the next, allowing for a larger contribution then as the room is cumulative. Unlike the RRSP, contributions to a TSFA do not result in an income tax deduction when they are made, but withdrawals are not reported as income. None of the earnings from the plan are included in income for any income-tested benefits, such as the Canada Child Tax Benefit or Goods and Services Tax Credit.

Consider the potential of making a contribution into the TFSA for each adult in the family:

- $5000 invested each year for a productive lifetime of 45 year (age 20 to 65) is $225,000.

- Add a compounding rate of return of 5% to this invested inside a tax-sheltered plan and that TFSA investment will grow to $838,426 inside the plan. By comparison, if this deposit had been invested outside the TFSA the amount would be only $547,420. The tax-free savings therefore are just over $290,000 or over twice as much more!

- At a 3% compounding interest rate, the accumulated capital would be $547,420 inside the TFSA, and only $376,253 outside of it, not as good, but still over $170,000 or 45% more in tax-free savings.

Don and Judy would have some time to shore up their investments for themselves, but using their children's time horizons, the family could accumulate much more wealth, on a tax-free basis. All Don and Judy need to do is to make sure everyone files a return and contributes to the TFSA—preferably at the maximum level—every year. Because the income accumulations will be tax-free, the pressure may be off Don to supplement his life insurance policy to shore up family wealth.

Here are some additional TFSA rules of note:

- **Basic investor profile:** Contributions can be made by/for those who have attained 18 years of age and are residents of Canada. There is no upper income limitation.

- **Earned income limitation:** There is no earned income limitation.

- **TFSA contribution room:** Every TFSA holder can contribute a maximum of $5000 per year, and this amount will be indexed after 2009, with rounding to the nearest $500.

- **Contribution deductibility:** Contributions to the account are not deductible.

- **Excess contributions:** These are subject to a 1% per month penalty until the amounts are removed.

- **Withdrawals (distributions)** of both earnings and principal are tax exempt.

- **Withdraw for any reason:** *Withdrawals (distributions) from the plan will create new TFSA contribution room.* Take the money out—principal and earnings—for what ever purpose you wish. Then you can put it back to grow again—you don't lose TFSA room once it is created.

- **Carry forward room:** Unused contribution room can be carried forward on an indefinite basis.

- **Income testing not affected:** Income-tested tax preferences like Child Tax Benefits, Employment Insurance Benefits or Old Age Security pension are not affected by earnings in the plan.

- **Attribution rules:** There is no attribution rule attached to the new TFSA, allowing parents and grandparents to transfer $5000 per year to each adult child in the family—for the rest of their lives. In addition, one spouse may transfer property into the TFSA of the other spouse without incurring attribution.

- **TFSA eligible investments:** The same eligible investments as allowed within an RRSP will apply to the TFSA. A special rule will prohibit a TFSA from making an investment in any entity with which the account holder does not deal at arm's length.

- **Interest deductibility:** Interest paid on money borrowed to invest in the TFSA is not deductible.

- **Stop Loss Rules:** A capital loss is denied when assets are disposed to a trust governed by an RRSP or RRIF. The same rule will be extended to investments disposed to a TFSA.

- **Use TFSA as security:** A TFSA may be used as security for a loan or other indebtedness.

- **Departure tax:** The TFSA is not caught by the departure tax rules. No TSFA contribution room is earned for those years where a person is non-resident and any withdrawals while non-resident cannot be replaced. The US does not recognize the TFSA, therefore any realized income should be non-taxable when removed after emigration. However, any capital appreciation will be taxable. Therefore it will make sense to remove capital properties from the TFSA on a tax-free basis immediately prior to emigrating to trigger the deemed disposition on a nominal gain on departure.

- **Marriage breakdown:** Upon breakdown of a marriage or common-law partnership, the funds from one party's TFSA may be transferred tax-free to the other party's TFSA. This will have no effect on the contribution room of either of the parties.

- **Death of a TFSA holder:** The funds within the account may be rolled over into their spouse's TFSA or they may be withdrawn tax-free. Any amounts earned within a TSFA after the death of the taxpayer are taxable to the estate.

See the Checklist of Investment Planning Ideas in the Summary of this chapter.

DEFER TAXABLE INCOME

Whenever you can defer paying tax, you should, to take advantage of the Time Value of Money. Another reason is to generate tax only when one anticipates a year when lower marginal tax rates will prevail.

A common way to do so is to invest in "registered" investment accounts. Although we have made reference to these investment products throughout this book, this is a good place to revisit their definitions and features. That's because, regardless of age or experience, the difference between a "registered" and a "non-registered" account is often misunderstood by novice investors.

When you invest in a **registered investment**, tax is never generated on investment income earned while the capital and earnings remain inside the registered plan. However, with the exception of accumulations in a TFSA, withdrawals of earnings, and in some cases, principal invested on a pre-tax basis are both fully taxable in the year of withdrawal, as described below:

- Taxable Principal and Earnings: RRSP, RRIF, RPP
- Taxable Earnings only: RESP, RDSP

Astutely timed to be withdrawn when the taxpayer is in a lower tax bracket (for example, upon retirement), taxes payable will be lower on the same amount of income than if earned while the investor's income was taxed at a higher marginal tax rate.

The most common registered investments, the Registered Retirement Savings Plan (RRSP), and for employees who belong to an employer-sponsored plan or Registered Pension Plan (RPP), both provide for a tax deduction when principal is invested, thereby reducing net income on the T1 Return. This will bring further gains in some tax brackets by way of increased social benefits and refundable tax credits, as described below.

Other registered investments defer tax without the benefit of a deduction for capital invested or the special treatment the TFSA offers. However, they are still important investment vehicles because they allow taxpayers to time income subject to tax: and in some cases, transfer income to other family members, or split income between spouses, depending on age.

You will notice reference to a new type of investment: the *Registered Disability Savings Plan (RDSP)*. This plan provides for the opportunity to save for a private pension specifically designed to suit the needs of disabled people who qualify for the Disability Tax Credit. Ask your tax advisors about this as an investment, structured much like an RESP (Registered Education Savings Plan) which features government contributions by way of a Registered Disability Savings Grant and Bond that sweeten the pot considerably.

Non-registered accounts

Income earned in non-registered accounts will be taxable, either now, or later. As described in earlier chapters, interest is the least tax-efficient source, dividends better (and sometimes best depending on your income range), and capital gains often best. This is because the taxpayer will not be taxed on accrued gains (value that is increasing) until the asset is disposed of (sold or transferred). In some cases, capital gains are exempt completely. Capital gains and losses are discussed in more detail in the next chapter.

BLENDING INCOME AND CAPITAL

When cash flow is an issue, it is possible, using some investment vehicles to create income that is a blend of capital and taxable earnings. The advantage of this is that the capital withdrawal is not immediately taxable, thereby increasing after-tax income. However, those capital withdrawals can later create a capital gain, as the adjusted cost base of the underlying asset must be reduced with every capital withdrawal. Examples of such investments include income trusts. Prescribed annuities also offer a blended income solution.

REDUCING TAX

It is always a primary concern of any tax-efficient investing strategy to create opportunities to reduce taxes each year. As we have seen, the RRSP can be used to both defer tax on investment income and reduce net income, which is very important, because net income (line 236 of the T1) is the figure used to limit the amount of social benefits taxpayers are entitled to (Old Age Security and Employment Insurance Benefits), and also to determine the level of refundable and non-refundable tax credits the family will receive. This includes the Child Tax Benefit and GST Credit as well as personal amounts.

We generally try to reduce taxes by focusing on the timing of taxable income resulting from the withdrawal of funds from registered accounts, reducing tax by splitting income and averaging withdrawals to take advantage of tax brackets and marginal rates.

Carrying Charges

There are also deductions available to reduce investment income, and the taxes payable. These amounts can be used to offset all other income of the year. The most common deductions for investment income that reduce taxes are carrying charges. These are expenses that an investor incurs to earn investment income and include the cost of interest on an investment loan, safety deposit box charges and investment counsel fees.

Tax Shelters

Tax shelters are a last resort. They provide tax deductions that can offset other income and in the case of certain flow through shares, can even create a tax exempt capital gain and a charitable donation credit, similar to the rules provided for donations of other publicly traded securities. But they are very risky. Speak to your tax and investment advisors.

Strategic Philanthropy

Investing in your community has tax benefits. Many people give at the door to their favorite registered charity. However, gifts of publicly traded shares provide significant tax benefits because accrued gains are tax-free when the shares are transferred to registered charities and private foundations (after March 19, 2007) It's important that those securities are transferred, not sold.

Zero income inclusion rates for purposes of capital gains and losses apply if you donate:

- Shares, debt obligations or rights listed on a designated stock exchange
- Shares of a mutual fund corporation
- Units of a mutual fund trust
- Interests in related segregated fund trusts
- Prescribed debt obligations
- Ecologically sensitive land

SHIFTING TAX

As we learned in the early chapter on family planning, a key strategy for tax-efficient investing is to take advantage of the ability to shift tax, where possible, to other related taxpayers (i.e. family members) who are in a lower marginal tax bracket. We can shift tax by planning adjusted cost base levels of capital assets with the opportunity to transfer assets to family members, particularly spouses. We also try to split investment income with family members, and use alternative structures like trusts and holding companies to maximize tax savings opportunities. As family wealth increases, your professional advisory team should be discussing these opportunities with you.

MINIMIZE INSTALMENT PAYMENTS

Most taxpayers have taxes deducted on their income sources—right off the top from their gross employment or pension earnings. *Some taxpayers have to make periodic remittances of taxes throughout the year, when taxes payable at tax filing time exceed a threshold of $3000 ($1800 in Quebec). Investors can often find themselves in this position. If you meet the profile, quarterly instalments are payable as follows:*

- *Individuals*—Generally, quarterly on March 15, June 15, September 15 and December 15.
- *Farmers and Fishers.* Individuals whose primary source of income is farming or fishing make one annual instalment payment (of at least 2/3 of the estimated taxes for the year) by December 31.

Always review your anticipated income level for the upcoming tax year carefully; instalments are based on your tax paying history. Write to the tax department to request a change in your previously determined payment schedule. Your tax professional can help you with the calculations. **Remember: Always pay yourself first. Avoid overpaying your taxes either by instalment or source deductions.**

MAKE THE LINK BETWEEN
INVESTMENT ACTIVITY AND TAXES

In planning for tax-efficient investment income, and the real goal, growth and preservation of after-tax capital, advisors and their clients should discuss income realization strategies. Selecting the right investment products to achieve the correct income results is important.

See the final chapter in this book for checklists and talking points you will want to discuss with your advisors.

IN SUMMARY

The new TFSA requires investors and their advisors to take a second look at the order in which they should maximize Real Wealth Management™ opportunities. Consider family priorities and then leverage the economic power available to you from inside and outside the family unit:

THINGS YOU NEED TO KNOW

Investment Product Selection—Order of Acquisition:

A. Registered Accounts:

- RPP: to maximize employer-sponsored contributions, claim deduction, shelter income
- RRSP: including spousal RRSP, to claim deduction and shelter income
- RESPs: to maximize Canada Education Savings Grants and Canada Learning Bonds
- RDSPs: to maximize Canada Disability Savings Grants & Canada Disability Savings Bonds
- TFSA: to earn tax exempt income and reusable contribution room

B. Non-registered Investments:

- Tax exempt principal residence
- Tax exempt insurance policies
- Non-registered investment accounts: focused on tax deferred and preferred investment income products that produce blended income and capital, capital gains, dividends and lastly interest.
- Strategic philanthropy

THINGS YOU NEED TO DO, QUESTIONS YOU NEED TO ASK, DECISIONS YOU NEED TO MAKE

Consider the following checklist planning opportunities to discuss with your professional advisory team, in order to make financial decisions around one key question: what comes first?

- **TFSA and RRSP:** Consider funding this new TFSA 'bucket of savings' with your RRSP tax savings—a great way to leverage two available tax provisions. But also look at your new investment options resulting from the accumulation of tax-exempt income within the TFSA. For example, it may make some sense funding the acquisition of assets that will multiply on a tax exempt basis or you might simply remove that money year over year to fund your new RRSP contribution room.

- **TFSA, RRSP or RPP?** Contributors to employer pension plans are often precluded from making RRSP contributions because of their pension adjustment amount. Likewise those who have contributed the maximum to an RRSP—18% of earned income to $20,000 in 2008 and want to do more to supplement their savings on a tax-assisted basis—now have the opportunity to tap into another tax deferred savings opportunity. In particular the TFSA is a good place to park interest-bearing investments.

- **TFSA with RRSP:** Executives who earn above the maximum earned income level for RRSP purposes will be unable to shelter more of their earnings for retirement. The TFSA provides a small window of opportunity to shore that tax assistance up. This option should be employed in conjunction with planning for Individual Pension Plans or Retirement Compensation Arrangements.

- **TFSAs and Pre-Retirees:** The TFSA is a great savings option for people who do not have the required earned income for RRSP contribution purposes and therefore have few opportunities for tax-sheltered retirement savings. Included are those in receipt of inactive income sources like pension income, investment income or employment insurance benefits.

- **TFSA and RRSP Age-Ineligible Taxpayers:** The tax shelter can continue for those who reach age 71 and don't need the money in their RRSP. While withdrawals must be generated under the usual rules, reinvestment into a TFSA will allow those tax-paid funds to grow again—faster—in a tax-sheltered account, as opposed to a non-registered account.

- **TFSA and RRSP Melt Down Strategy:** It has always made some sense to melt down RRSPs to "top income up to bracket" in circumstances where taxes will be higher at death than during life. We generally use that strategy for singles or widow(er)s for example. Now surplus funds can be deposited into the TFSA so that retirees can continue to build wealth on a tax deferred basis and keep legacies intact.

- **TFSA or RESP?** Is the TFSA a better savings vehicle for education purposes than the RESP (Registered Education Savings Plan)? Not on the first $2500 of contributions. This should be deposited to an RESP to generate a government grant called the Canada Education Savings Grant and potentially a Canada Learning Bond. However, after this, the money should go into the TFSA for tax-free savings. The RESP does provide a tax penalty on withdrawal if intended recipients do not end up going to school.

- **TFSA or RDSP?** The new Registered Disability Savings Plan features components similar to the RESP. Its purpose is to help the community to fund pensions for people who qualify for the Disability Tax Credit. It is a powerful investment by itself because every contribution can earn either a three-to-one or two-to-one matching grant or bond.

- **TFSA or HBP?** Consider whether it makes more sense to withdraw funds on a tax-free basis from within an RRSP to fund a new home purchase under the Home Buyers' Plan or whether the taxpayer save and withdraw funds under the TFSA instead. As there are no tax penalties for failure to pay back the funds to the TFSA, and withdrawals automatically create new TFSA contribution room, it may make sense to accumulate money in the TFSA instead.

- **TFSA or LLP?** Education savings strategies should now be revisited as well. Saving within the TFSA allows you to accumulate funds on a tax-deferred basis and then withdraw them without penalty or a requirement to repay the funds. This is not so under the Lifelong Learning Plan, which allows for a tax-free withdrawal from the RRSP but requires an annual repayment schedule. The avoidance of income inclusion penalties therefore makes the TFSA a more attractive withdrawal vehicle.

- **TFSA vs. Non-Registered Accounts:** Because income from the TFSA is not taxable, borrowing funds to contribute to a TFSA will not be tax deductible. Using borrowed money to invest in non-registered accounts makes more sense as interest is then tax deductible.

MASTER YOUR TAXES
On Your Investments

TIPS

- Tax-efficient investing requires an understanding of the marginal tax rates each type of investment income earned is subject to.
- The basic strategies for tax-efficient investing include strategies to avoid tax, defer tax, blend income and capital, reduce tax, and shift tax to lower taxing environments.
- Selecting investment products to achieve the correct income results is important.
- Every investment planning strategy follows the same basic pattern for each individual in the family; then the results for the family must be considered:
  - Identify current marginal tax rates for investor and family members.
  - Identify taxable income sources for each member of the family.
  - Identify marginal tax rate for each source of income to be generated.
  - Take measures to capitalize on personal tax-free zones, average down taxes paid on family income sources with income splitting.
- Where investment income that would be taxed currently at a high marginal rate can be earned tax-free, or deferred until a later year when the marginal tax rate would be lower, the tax advantages can be significant, particularly when you view that opportunity within the context of the economic power of family, employer, and community (through tax-assisted giving).

TRAPS

- **Don't miss filing a tax return:** A tax return is required to build both TFSA and RRSP contribution room so it is folly to file late or miss filing a return. Don't cut into your tax exempt and tax deferred wealth accumulation potential by being tardy on this front.

CHAPTER 7

Finances: Managing Dispositions of Your Assets

We simply attempt to be fearful when others are greedy and to be greedy only when others are fearful. WARREN BUFFETT

"With all the volatility in the world today, one of the things I am very happy about is that we taught our children how to save." Madeline was visiting her mom, still vibrant, working in her rose garden. "I have heard of so many who took losses over the years, but you know Mom, you and Dad were right. When you know how to save, there is always a little rainbow in the house, with a pot of gold at the end of it."

"Madeline, my grandchildren deserve credit for their young stewardship and so do you for guiding them," Vivienne smiled with pride. "They are responsible people who are not wasteful, and that will really pay off for them, especially with today's real estate and stock market turmoil."

"I have to hand it to Victoria," laughed Marilyn thinking about her precocious 18 year old. "She really gets it! She actually passed up that trip to Mexico with her girlfriends, and made her first $1000 deposit into a TFSA today! She has her heart set on that cute downtown condo…and she just might be able afford it, too, with all her tax smarts!"

THE ISSUES

Fear and greed. One drive prices up, the other drives them down. These are the two emotions that make for fascinating bull and bear markets. To get the results you want in either trend, timing, of course, is everything. Disciplined, strategic, knowledgeable and often lucky investors sell at the top of a cycle and buy at the bottom. However, they also pause long enough, before crystallizing either euphoric gains or staggering losses, to understand the real dollar effect of their actions.

Selling is permanent, and it comes with tax consequences. These consequences can work in your favor to average out your both gains and losses and position you for the next financial construction site. Acquisitions require savings...or the ability to borrow...which is based on your credit-worthiness. Again, a sharp tax eye can put you in the driver's seat sooner.

But in the end, cashing out may have absolutely nothing to do with the current real estate or stock market. The disposition of your assets—by sale or transfer—may be voluntary or involuntary, because life happens: marriage, divorce, births or deaths, disability or retirement.

When you combine the two sets of knowledge—skillful saving and strategic selling—with a sharp knowledge of the tax consequences, you are in a position of control to build your family's net worth. And in the end, that's the issue, isn't it?

THE SOLUTIONS

In the last chapter we showed you how to save from a tax-efficiency point of view. When you work with a tax or financial advisor in planning your investments, your retirement or your estate, two themes should always emerge: you need a strategy (mission, vision and goals) and you need an action plan (the right products, services and people to take you to your destination).

Saving is easier when you have goals and you do it regularly and with consistency. It also helps to measure your savings against your mission, vision and goals. One way to do this is to regularly assess your financial position—your personal net worth. A good time to do this is when you prepare your annual tax return.

The tax preparation exercise is a good one from the point of view of understanding the family's personal Income and Expense Statements. That burdensome documentation assembly process, which we'll help you master in a later chapter, is necessary for tax compliance reasons, but also, if done well, for the purpose of helping you revisit your required after-tax cash flow. Filing a tax return also provides you with the opportunity to qualify to save new capital on a tax-sheltered basis. This of course refers to RRSP and TFSA contribution room.

When you have this tax information, together with an understanding of your financial position, you are well positioned to save more money and build more real wealth.

HOW TO SAVE

To build real wealth, it is important to know how to save at every juncture on a tax-efficient basis. Regardless of age or lifecycle, there is never a good reason not to have an ongoing savings plan. In fact, in a typical retirement period of 20 years, many seniors find they can save a lot.

Consider putting away $100 a month at an average 7% return at age 20, and you'll end up with just under $400,000 at age 65. However, if you waited to age 60, and started to save $100 a month for 15 years, you'd only have about $30,000 more capital. If you save in tax-preferred or tax deferral vehicles, reinvesting tax dollars saved in planning, while reducing fees for investing, it's possible to double and even tripled your available capital. Despite the fact that s/he may have squandered valuable saving time as a youth, even an early retiree can still make significant progress and accumulate savings that exceed what most people have in their retirement savings today.

No matter what your age is today, and no matter how well or poorly you fared in the latest bear market, to shore up capital and use the power of compounding time to build a new or bigger nest egg, consider discussing the following with your family and advisors:

1. How to budget to save more every month.
2. How to cut corners, spend less and more astutely.
3. How to work more and for more money.
4. How to invest with tax-efficiency and consistency.
5. How to realize more after-tax dollars on asset dispositions with proper planning.

HOW TO CAPITALIZE ON YOUR INCOME-PRODUCING INVESTMENTS

Assets which have been held to produce income or appreciate will at some time be sold or otherwise disposed of, often generating a capital gain; sometimes a capital loss. Capital gains are subject to preferred tax treatment. We will take a closer look at how to maximize these opportunities; however, a clarification is necessary before we begin.

Capital gains and losses earned inside a registered account will lose their identity. For example when you earn a capital gain in your RRSP, the gain is added to the value of the plan, but later, upon withdrawal of the funds, the full amount of principal and earnings are taxable.

Therefore, it may be good to hold assets that produce capital treatment outside your registered accounts if you want to benefit from the preferred tax treatment. This is generally true except for investments in a Tax-Free Savings Account. In that case, all resulting income, including capital gains is tax exempt.

The discussion below takes a general approach for the purposes of understanding how the acquisition and disposition of assets can affect net worth and cash flow from a tax point of view. The topic is detailed and can be complicated, and so the hope is that the information will arm you with enough information to ask better questions of your financial advisors resulting in more knowledgeable decision making.

Tax Consequences on the Sale of Income-Producing Assets

To understand the tax consequences that could occur when you sell an income-producing asset, it is important to understand what a capital gain is. Simply put, a capital gain arises when an asset is disposed of for more than its adjusted cost base. In an equation, the calculation looks like this:

Capital Gain = Proceeds of Disposition − Adjusted Cost Base

Actual vs. Deemed Dispositions

This simple definition requires some explanation of the terms; for example, many people can understand that a capital gain may happen upon a sale of an asset. That is included in the definition of "proceeds of disposition." In that case, money changes hands between a seller and a buyer.

However, a tax consequence also may occur when there is a "deemed disposition." That is, a taxable event is considered to have happened in these circumstances:

- At death
- Upon transfer of the asset as a gift
- When property is transferred to a trust
- When a taxpayer emigrates (becomes a non-resident of Canada)
- If the asset is damaged or destroyed

In these situations, the proceeds of disposition will generally be the Fair Market Value (FMV) of the asset at the time of disposition. This is important, as an appraisal is necessary to justify that valuation for tax purposes.

In a previous chapter you learned that when it comes to real estate held by a taxpayer for personal use and enjoyment, the gains on the disposition of a property designated as the principal residence will not be taxable.

If the taxpayer converts that personal use property to an income producing property, a change in use will generally be deemed to have occurred.

In that case of such a "deemed disposition", a taxable consequence based on the FMV of the property at the time of the change must be reported, although some optional elections may defer the actual payment of taxes.

What is Adjusted Cost Base?

The Adjusted Cost Base (ACB) of an asset is its tax cost. It is made up of:

- the asset's actual cost or FMV (in the case of a deemed acquisition) as at the time of acquisition, plus
- the cost of improvements to the property (but not repairs).

This latter point is important. The ACB of the property can be increased by costs incurred to improve the useful life of the property. This is different from repairs, which restore the asset to its original condition. An example of a capital addition to the cost base of a revenue property, for example, would be the cost of a new roof, a new deck, landscaping or a boat house. An example of a repair would be the replacement of shingles, or maintenance like the painting of a fence.

Valuation Days

There is one more thing you need to know about calculating Proceeds of Disposition and Adjusted Cost Base of an asset for tax purposes: the length of time the asset has been held will affect its cost base. Special rules exist for the calculation of ACB for taxpayers who owned capital property on a "Valuation Day".

Did you know there was no capital gains tax in Canada before 1972? The cost base to the taxpayer who has owned an asset prior to this will calculate its cost based on the "median" value of:

- The cost of the asset
- The V-Day value of the asset
- The proceeds of disposition

Other valuation days are possible when the asset being disposed of is a principal residence.

Calculating the Taxable Capital Gain

Once we know what the right figures are for Proceeds of Disposition and the Adjusted Cost Base, we can calculate the capital gain on the sale of our asset. The ACB is simply subtracted from the net proceeds of disposition. We can also deduct any cost of making the sale, like commissions or appraisals, for example.

Next, we need to determine how much of this is taxable. Today, for most assets, 50% of the gain is included in income as the "taxable capital gain".

However, that income inclusion rate of 50% was not always so: as you know, capital gains were not taxable at all prior to 1972; and since then, various governments have tinkered with the inclusion rates so that the history of the capital gains inclusion rates looks like this:

- $1/2$ (50%) for transactions after December 31, 1971 and before January 1, 1988 and after October 17, 2000.

- $2/3$ (66 2/3%) for transactions after December 31, 1987 and before January 1, 1990 and after February 28, 2000 and before October 18, 2000.

- $3/4$ (75%) for transactions after December 31, 1989 and before February 29, 2000.

- Zero inclusion rate: where a taxpayer donates certain listed securities or an ecological property to a registered charity after May 2, 2006, (or similar entity other than a private foundation), the capital gains inclusion rate is zero.

Example: Jason sold publicly traded shares

Jason sold some of his publicly traded shares at the start of the year and realized a capital gain of $150,000. What is the taxable capital gain?

Answer: The taxable capital gain is $75,000 (= $1/2$ of $150,000)

Assume the same facts as above, but this time, assume that Jason donated shares to a registered charity. What is the taxable capital gain?

Answer: The taxable capital gain is $0. That's because Jason can roll over or transfer the shares on a tax-free basis to his favourite charity and avoid including the taxable gain realized on the transfer in income. He will also receive a charitable donation receipt for FMV of the transferred shares, which will reduce his taxes payable.

What Happens When There is a Loss?

A capital loss occurs when an income-producing asset is sold, or deemed to have been disposed of, for less than the total of its adjusted cost base (ACB) and outlays and expenses on disposition.

This is important: any capital losses incurred will offset capital gains earned in the year, but generally not other income.

There is more good news: if losses exceed gains in the current year they may be carried back to any of the previous three years or forward to any subsequent year, to offset capital gains reported in those year. That's a great way to reach back and recover taxes previously reported as a result of a bull market!

And if you don't have any capital gains this year or the previous three and never have another capital gain as long as you live (don't worry things will likely turn around!), here's what you need to know: don't make the mistake of not reporting your net capital losses. Those losses will offset all other income in the year of death and in the immediately preceding tax year. They are therefore valuable and no matter how unpleasant this may seem to you, 'fess up at tax time, okay?

Tax Loss Selling

At year end it is not unusual for investors and their advisors to review portfolios for the purpose of offsetting capital gains of the prior three years with capital losses of the current year. This is an important way to average down the taxes paid on capital appreciation and increase cash flow used to reinvest or pay down debt. Speak to your tax and financial advisors to prepare the right formula for loss realization: one that provides a refund in the prior year in which the highest tax liabilities occurred.

Capital Properties are Not All the Same

Capital properties are classified into different categories for the purposes of claiming gains and losses. Real estate, as you know, may be classified as a personal use property, if it was used as personal residence by its owner. Upon disposition of personal-use real estate, like all other personal-use property except for the tax exempt principal residence, gains must be included in income as capital gains, but losses are deemed to be nil.

Depreciable Properties

It is important to note, that depreciable assets will be treated differently, also. A depreciable asset might be a piece of machinery used in business or a revenue property. While gains in value over the cost of the asset are reported in a similar fashion to all other properties, losses in value are generally written off on the business statement as a deduction.

In some other cases, special rules apply to the calculation and application of capital losses; for example, you might wish to ask your tax advisor about Listed Personal Property Losses, Limited Partnership Losses, Business Investment Losses, Losses on Labour-Sponsored Funds, Stop Loss Rules, and Superficial Losses.

Calculating the Real Dollar Fallout

The amount of taxes actually payable on the capital gain included in your income will depend on your tax bracket and your marginal tax rate, using both federal and provincial tax rates. Check this out with your tax advisor.

Excluded Property

The following types of property are explicitly excluded from the definition of capital property so that no gain or loss on such property is ever a capital gain or loss:

- Eligible Capital Property;
- Cultural Property;
- Resource Property;

- Specified Debt Obligations;
- Insurance Policies (except related segregated fund trusts);
- Timber Resource Properties.

The Capital Gains Deduction

Here is some more good news, especially for family business owners. Every individual is allowed to have a $750,000 lifetime Capital Gains Deduction. This deduction is claimed in computing taxable income, and will shelter from tax a gain on the disposition of certain eligible property. This includes:

- shares of a qualified small business corporation,
- qualified farm property or
- qualified fishing property disposed of on or after May 2, 2006.

A taxpayer's ability to access this deduction can be affected by business investment losses claimed in either the current or prior years, and by something known as CNIL: cumulative net investment losses in excess of investment income after 1988.

The deduction is limited to $500,000 for gains arising from dispositions before March 19, 2007. The additional $250,000 is available to offset gains realized after March 18, 2007. From a planning perspective, it is important to make sure as many people in the family as possible will qualify for a capital gains deduction by virtue of their ownership. It is also possible to multiply access to the capital gains deduction by using a family trust. Be sure to discuss these lucrative options for realizing tax-free gains on business succession, with your advisors.

The $100,000 Capital Gains Election

Prior to February 22, 1994, a $100,000 general capital gains deduction was available; however it was repealed on that date. Taxpayers were allowed a one-time opportunity to "use up" any remaining $100,000 capital gains deduction they may have had by electing to increase the adjusted cost base (ACB) of capital property on hand up to the $100,000 level.

This was accomplished by making an election to report a capital gain based upon the fair market value (FMV) of the eligible assets held on February 22, 1994. CRA Form T664 was used to do so.

With the exception of flow-through entities when the election was made, the taxpayer was deemed to have disposed of the capital asset at the elected amount and to have then immediately re-acquired it. *That means the ACB of the asset became the elected amount.*

Here's why this is important to you and anyone who might be an executor of an estate: any subsequent disposition of assets affected must take the elected amount into account when determining the ACB. If you don't do this, you'll likely calculate a capital gain that is too high and as a result pay too much tax on the disposition.

Be sure to find a copy of Form T664 if you think you or the deceased taxpayer you may be the executor for may have made this election.

Deducting the Cost of Interest

Tax-efficient investing, from a leverage point of view, involves carefully constructing the financial picture to make any interest paid on loans taken for investment purposes deductible as a "carrying charge". These deductions fully offset other income of the year. There are some special rules taxpayers must observe for this to happen, however:

- **Interest on Capital Gains Producing Assets.** Interest on funds borrowed to invest are deductible when they are made to earn income. In cases of investments in interest and dividend producing investments, the "purpose of earning income from property" is easily met. However, when money is borrowed to invest in shares that have no potential for income from property—dividends, for example, interest costs will not be deductible.

- **Separate Personal Interest from Investment Interest.** It is critical that the interest on the investment portion of any loan or line of credit be separately tracked from capital used for personal purposes.

- **Deduct Investment Interest on Diminished Assets.** Interest deductibility may continue as long as the investment continues to be owned. This is an important tip where the investment has diminished in value. Continue to track interest expenses and claim them as a carrying charge.
- **Interest Costs on Segregated Funds.** Note that when an investor borrows to make a segregated fund purchase, the interest on the loan will be tax-deductible according to normal rules, despite the fact that this is an insurance-based product. Normally, interest on money borrowed to invest in an insurance policy is not deductible.

Ready, Set, Build Wealth

Taken together with the information you learned about tax-efficient investing within a family context in prior chapters, you are now equipped to ask the right questions of your advisors as you deliberate decision making about how to build new wealth in an extremely interesting time.

Remember fear occurs when we don't know what will happen next. Sometimes it pays to wait on the sidelines, saving money tax efficiently and with consistent discipline to be ready to travel on, once the fog subsides.

Remember, success is what happens when opportunity meets preparedness.

Then there is the question of greed. What can we say? Greed is bad... checks and balances are good. That's why you should spend more time choosing your tax and financial advisors carefully. You want to work with people who are honest, caring stewards of your family's wealth. A good way to find them is to check for their take on strategy, process and plan.

IN SUMMARY

In summarizing this chapter we want to think about the future of economic activity and to do so, we look to words of wisdom from Robert Ironside, ABD, Ph.D., co-author of the certificate course Portfolio Construction for Real Wealth Management, published by The Knowledge Bureau:

Extensive research has shown that active management rarely adds value over long periods of time and in most cases simply reduces the total return available to the investor. Based on this evidence, what simple rules can be devised to ensure that both investors and their Advisors make the best possible investment decisions to accumulate real wealth? Here are eight rules:

1. Invest only in low-cost assets and hold them for long periods of time.

2. Invest only in funds with low asset turnover, to minimize transaction costs.

3. Invest early and often—time is the investor's greatest ally.

4. Change the asset mix between high-risk, high return equities and lower-risk, lower-return bonds and Treasury Bills to achieve the right risk profile.

5. Don't allow market ups and downs to change your investment philosophy.

6. Rebalance the portfolio back to the benchmark asset class weights on a periodic basis. This involves selling the high-return asset and investing the proceeds in the low-return asset.

7. Focus only on the real rate of return.

8. Tax-efficiency is important.

THINGS YOU NEED TO KNOW

- Selling is permanent, and it comes with tax consequences.
- Capital gains or losses can result from actual dispositions or deemed dispositions.
- Valuations of your assets may be necessary upon acquisition or disposition.
- Capital losses will offset capital gains, in the current and three immediately prior tax years. Carrying back losses can generate new cash flow from tax refunds.
- Unused capital loss balances may eventually offset all other income on your final tax return, and the immediately preceding year, so make sure this information is retrievable.
- You cannot claim losses on the sale of your personal residences.
- Shareholders in a qualified small business corporation may earn $750,000 in tax-free gains on the disposition of their shares.
- Executors need to take into account the value of elected assets of February 22, 1994 when they are filing final returns.

THINGS YOU NEED TO DO

- Use the annual tax filing and documentation ritual to determine your personal net worth.
- Apply capital losses against capital gains to get a return on your losers.
- Capital loss balances are reported on your Notice of Assessment or Reassessment from the CRA. Keep that information in your permanent tax records in a safe place.
- Dig out your capital gains election form from February 22, 1994 and file it with your will so that you executors don't over report capital gains on your elected assets.

QUESTIONS YOU NEED TO ASK

- Did I have any capital gains in the past three years?

DECISIONS YOU NEED TO MAKE

- Should I generate losses by selling assets to offset those gains and recoup some taxes paid?

MASTER YOUR TAXES
Your Assets: Managing Dispositions

TIPS

- Investing in income producing assets can be very tax-efficient.
- Accrued gains in your assets will not be taxed until disposition.
- Upon disposition only 50% of gains are taxable.
- Gains on the shares of publicly traded securities can be avoided entirely when they are donated by way of transfer to your favorite charity.
- Gains on the disposition of a principal residence are tax exempt, too.
- Capital losses will reduce capital gains of the current year.
- Excess losses can be carried back and carried forward to save more tax dollars.
- Capital gains become taxable in 1972; assets that have been held since that time may be subject to appraisal as of certain valuation days.
- Capital gains and losses earned inside a registered plan will lose their identity, so it may be best to hold these assets outside your RRSP if you want to benefit from the preferred tax treatment.

TRAPS

- Don't miss filing a tax return to record capital losses.
- Don't miss adjusting your prior filed returns to carry back excess losses; you'll loose out on new cash flow.
- Interest costs relating to capital assets will only be deductible if there is the potential for income from property. Discuss these traps with your advisors.

Principle Mastery: Tax-efficient asset dispositions can backfill the uncontrollables in life and in the marketplace. It is your right to arrange your affairs to pay the least tax possible and when it comes to capital dispositions, you are often in control of timing, which can help average up the losses in market with tax savings.

CHAPTER 8

Future:
Transitioning into Retirement

It is impossible to walk rapidly and be unhappy. MOTHER TERESA

"This is really scary," Guy shook his head as he reviewed his investment portfolio. Fluctuations in the stock market had taken his money for a real ride; a swooning roller coaster of ups and downs that eroded his confidence for his family's financial security.

His partner of 30 years, Samantha was just as concerned. "I heard today that my company may not have enough in its reserves to meet its funding requirements for our company pension plan. What are we going to do if our pension doesn't come through for us?"

"Thank goodness we have our savings in the RRSP and a fully paid home," said Guy, "and thank goodness we have our health and each other. We'll make it through—we always have—it just may be a bit different than we envisioned."

THE ISSUES

Why is retirement income planning so mystical for most? It's almost as mind boggling as doing income tax returns! After a lifetime of hard work, dedicated savings and an incredible work ethic, the number one issue still seems to be: will I have enough to retire?

It is actually surprising that so many seasoned, experienced and successful people have trouble with this question. After all, many tackled a far more overwhelming challenge earlier in life: the raising of educated children through career, financial and relationship obstacles, most *having no capital at all* when they started this journey as young parents. The plan for retirement generally begins with at least some savings and some income from various retirement plans.

The significant issue for many, who near the end of their work life, is understanding first the loss of control over income generation, to rely on pensions and other accumulations to continue with lifestyle. This is especially so after the financial meltdown of a lifetime, which began in the fall of 2008. A testament to their uneasiness, pre-retirees buckled down to work more, longer and harder to make up for the losses in their retirement portfolios.

How does one come to trust a volatile marketplace to achieve peace of mind while living on a fixed income? It's possible, and even powerful, but it's not mystical. Retirement planning is simply the continuation of your careful management of resources. The wildcards are just different: your health, your mortality, your purchasing power and the performance of your investments may be out of your direct control. However, your spending and saving habits are, and enhanced by tax-efficiency can diversify away those risks. Mastering your taxes can help.

THE SOLUTIONS

A successful retirement is the culmination of a lifetime of personal productivity. It is a great time to continue the real wealth management process—the stewardship of after-tax, inflation-protected capital—now to be used for a different purpose.

In earlier chapters we identified the resources of most value to most people: time and money. Retirement income needs must be met while keeping an eye on the successful transition of a smartly accruing portfolio to fund the needs of future generations. We don't subscribe to the notion "spend it all before you die." That's imprudent and wasteful.

Indeed when there is a mission and vision for the future, coupled with careful stewardship, retirement is just a small, yet significant phase, in the continued life of your capital. That's an important concept, because your focus on continued real wealth management—after tax, inflation and costs—will result in peace of mind.

When it comes to relying on passive, fixed income to fund needs, it is important to always be prepared. Consider the greatest threats to retirement in planning for it: lower than projected investment returns, erosion of capital, higher than projected inflation and unforeseen expenses that erode cash flow, including high medical expenses and taxes.

The process you employ to manage these threats is important. Budgeting and forecasting is important and wants and needs are likely best identified in a series of 3 to 5 year stages. By doing so savings accumulated before and during retirement can actually continue to grow.

Fortunately, there are some consistent funding sources for retirement: public pension plans are one good example. The combined maximum benefits of the Canada Pension Plan and the Old Age Security are now about $17,000 per person; or $1400 a month before tax; enough to keep most seniors who have worked during their lifetime, above the poverty line, even in expensive urban centres. Many will have private pension or investment sources above this.

One could certainly move to a warm, third world country and live really well with that kind of a draw, at least at the start of the retirement journey. But that's not realistic for many, who will need to tap into Canada's health care system and, from a personal point of view, want to be nearer to the family and its traditions at the end of the retirement period.

Planning for this journey is really about developing a vision, re-examining what's important to you and working within a new budget. You will need to manage income and expenditure patterns, and retire debt. You may also begin a new relationship with the government too, as you may find yourself remitting tax by instalment for the first time. There are six steps to consider in doing all of this on a tax-efficient basis:

1. Planning Tax-Efficient Transitions from Employment
2. Maximizing Employer Funded Pensions
3. Maximizing Private Pensions
4. Reaping the Most from Public Pensions
5. Investment Income Planning
6. Managing Tax Instalments

PLANNING TAX-EFFICIENT TRANSITIONS FROM EMPLOYMENT

The number of seniors in Canada is projected to grow from 4.2 million to 9.8 million between 2005 and 2036, largely representing the boomer population. These, of course, are the people who are worried today about whether they can retire, given the serious financial crisis being experienced at the doorstep of this new stage of life.

To bring context to the planning process, it helps to understand some of the parameters recent history provides us with, based on a July 2007 report from Human Resources Development Canada:

- **Median retirement age:** The median age of retirement in Canada is 61.0; that is, 62.6 for men and 60.0 for women (2005). This is somewhat higher than in 1997, when the median retirement age hit a low of 60.6.

- **Life expectancy:** Life expectancy in Canada for both sexes combined surpassed 80 years for the first time—80.2 years. Life expectancy for men was 77.8 years and for women it was 82.6. However, differences in life expectancy have begun to narrow since that statistic was established in 2004 and gender composition is expected to become more even amongst seniors.

- **Median retirement income planning period:** This means that the average length of retirement for which income must be planned is 19 years.

- **Seniors in the workplace:** According to the *Organisation for Economic Co-operation and Development (OECD) Thematic Review of Older Workers*, 2005, older workers in Canada are faring well in the labour market. They have higher than average earnings and lower than average unemployment rates.

- **Seniors and unemployment:** The bad news, however is that individuals aged 55-64 who lose their jobs stay unemployed, on average, for nearly 50% longer than prime-age workers. Older workers in remote and/or one-industry communities are especially at risk in the event of layoff or firm closure.

So the economic reality for most boomers is a transition out the work-force, rather than an entry into retirement on a "cold turkey" basis. From a planning perspective this means that there will be many "layers" of income, particularly at the start of retirement. The goal is to receive them tax efficiently, identify those tax efficiencies, and reinvest them.

Your retirement income buckets will therefore be comprised of:

1. Income from actively earned sources: employment or self-employment
2. Income from Employer-Funded Superannuation (RPPs—Registered Pension Plans)
3. Income from private pension savings (RRSPs (Registered Retirement Savings Plans), RRIFs (Registered Retirement Income Plans) or other annuities that pay benefits periodically)
4. Retirement benefits from the CPP (Canada Pension Plan)
5. Retirement benefits from the OAS (Old Age Security)
6. Investment sources: hopefully all of the income sources mentioned above will be withdrawn to fund personal living needs well before you need to tap into any other investments. However, if you must, there is a most tax-efficient basis to do so; often without generating any taxable income at all.

Maximizing Active Income Sources

Remember that income from employment or self-employment may continue on a consulting or part-time basis for many years to come. You may find those sources will be taxed more advantageously now that you are in a lower tax bracket.

In addition, until you are age-ineligible (72) a portion of that income can be and likely should be tax-sheltered with RRSP contributions. Most people will still bear marginal tax rates of between twenty and fifty cents on every dollar they earn. You just can't afford not to take that double digit return the RRSP generates in tax savings.

And, there are some new options for tax-efficient savings that can really help prepare you for retirement, and in retirement to. Therefore tax savings generated by the RRSP contribution and deduction could be leveraged to help you save even more.

The TFSA

A keen focus on the time value of money, supplemented by tax savings, can now be added to a new pot. Starting in January 2009, every Canadian resident who files a tax return creates $5000 in unused TFSA room, so that you can deposit money in a **Tax-Free Savings Account**. The name says it all.

The bucket to tap to fund "mad money"—exotic trips, special gifts to grandchildren, or short term living costs due to unstable financial markets—has just grown. Not only will you be earn investment income completely tax-free in this account, but there is absolutely no tax cost to taking money out of a TFSA. This means you can supplement extra wants or needs from this account with complete tax-efficiency.

You will want to run to your tax practitioner's office every tax season to file that return so that you can max-fund both an RRSP and a TFSA. There are many ways to do that, even in pre- and post-retirement. Tax savings due to pension income splitting can be a primary source, for example.

MAXIMIZING EMPLOYER-FUNDED PENSIONS

Benefits received as superannuation from an employer-funded pension are taxable and qualify for a $2000 pension income amount on the personal tax return each year. Before leaving your employment, however, it is important to know about three specific opportunities that can help you leverage your company pension significantly:

1. pension income splitting
2. phased in retirement
3. transfers of RRSP accumulations into an RPP

1. Pension Income Splitting

Starting in January 2007, Canadian retirees can split up to 50% of pension income received from various private pension sources; however, the rules are somewhat skewed in favor of those who have employer-sponsored plans. That's because qualifying pension income for these purposes is linked to the taxpayer's eligibility for the $2000 pension income amount on line 314 of the tax return.

Specifically, superannuation received on a periodic basis from an employer-sponsored plan is an eligible source for pension income splitting *at any age*; while periodic pension income received from an RRSP or RRIF is not, until the age of 65.

(It would therefore be good for the self-employed, who need to rely on their RRSP accumulations to fund retirement, to consider starting an employer-funded pension plan within their companies well before retirement to take advantage of the lucrative results pension income splitting can bring.)

In fact, the pension income splitting opportunity puts the RPP first on the list of "pension income buckets". Pension income provides:

- an additional tax-free zone (the $2000 pension income amount for each person, over and above the Basic Personal Amount) and
- averages tax downward on the superannuation itself, taking full advantage of our progressive tax system.

In fact if the spouse to which the income is being split is under age 65 and has no other income, s/he will be able to receive about $1000 a month tax-free (sheltered by the $10,100 Basic Personal Amount and $2000 for the pension income amount).

That's a simply great way to add to your capital accumulations while you enjoy tax-free cash flow! Consider this planning example for Guy and Samantha who are age 65 and 66 respectively and live on Guy's superannuation of $2000 a month, as well as receiving maximum benefits from the CPP and OAS: pension income splitting saves this family about $1200 a year.

Now consider the potential for capital accumulation by investing those savings in a TFSA every year for the entire retirement period Samantha is planning for. Capital accumulations—even before tax-free investment income is earned—will be close to $23,000. Considering that the median net worth of Canadians in the 65 plus age category is $155,000, this single income tax provision has increased this family's net worth in the retirement period, by almost 15%! And that's before any tax-free investment income growth.

2. Phased-in Company Pensions

To make sure qualifying pension income is generated to maximize these income splitting advantages, use another new provision available to those age 55 or older: phased-in pensions. An employee is able to draw up to 60% of the benefits that have otherwise accrued under the employer-sponsored pension plan while continuing to accumulate benefits based on current employment, provided that the employee is at least 55. No conditions are imposed on whether the employee works part- or full-time.

That means you can work part time, draw up to 60% of your superannuation, split the income with your spouse and pay a low rate of tax, all the while continuing to accrue pension benefits. That's a great use of tax-efficiency. It makes sense to take the opportunity to generate income in two hands rather than just one. Later in retirement you just may not have that chance.

3. Transfer of funds from a taxpayer's RRSP

It is possible to transfer capital accumulated within an RRSP on a tax-free basis to an RPP that you may be a member of. Given that you'll have to wait to qualify for the opportunity for pension income splitting until age 65 if your money stays in the RRSP, this can make absolute sense. Form T2033 may be used to affect the transfer. Check with your payroll department to make sure the terms of the RPP will allow this.

However, remember, this has to happen while you are still a member of the pension plan.

BENEFITS FROM PRIVATE PENSIONS

As you know, an RRSP is a tax-assisted retirement savings plan, contributions to which are based on an individual's "unused contribution room." This room can only be created by filing a tax return, yet so many people are chronic late filers and if you are in that group as you near retirement, you'll want to that cleared up. The amount of the "room" acknowledged by CRA is reported on the taxpayer's personal Notices of Assessment or Reassessment, based on the results on the T1 Return, and in the absence of it, you'll underfund your RRSP and with it an opportunity to split private pension income with your spouse. There are four main benefits to making an RRSP contribution:

- A tax deduction is allowed for the RRSP contribution made to the plan, up to your available contribution room. That deduction will reduce the taxpayer's net income.

- The reduction in net income will reduce taxes payable. Where applicable, the reduction in a taxpayer's net income will also increase social benefits received from federal and provincial refundable tax credits or the Old Age Security, by decreasing clawbacks. Retirees want to plan to receive all the credits and benefits they possibly can and an RRSP can help.

- The income earned on the principal invested loses its identity within the plan, in that the whole amount—principal and earnings—will be taxed as income on withdrawal. However, while in the plan, the earnings are not taxable, providing for a tax deferral.

- The tax savings generated by the RRSP contribution can be leveraged. As we saw in the example above, deposits to a TFSA make the most sense first, as they can accumulate tax-free forever—there is no upper age barrier.

A taxpayer's contribution room is decreased by any RRSP contributions deducted in the year. If the contribution room earned is not used in the year, the unused RRSP contribution room may be accumulated and carried forward for use in the future. This includes periods of time when you are no longer age-eligible to make contributions.

There is no lower age limit for contributing to an RRSP; however, the RRSP must be collapsed by the end of the year in which the taxpayer turns 71. Therefore, in addition to the requirement for contribution room, in order to be eligible to contribute to his own RRSP, a taxpayer must be under 71 years of age.

Collapsing RRSPs

Money can be taken out of the RRSP at any time, but when it is, both earnings and principal will be taxable. Unfortunately there is no tax relief until the taxpayer turns 65, or receives the amounts as a result of a spouse's death. When that criteria is met, the income can be offset with a $2000 pension income amount. That amount can be transferred to a spouse, or pension income splitting may be applied.

When the RRSP eligible age limit (71) is reached, a pension must be generated. There are several options for creating income and further deferral of tax on the earnings. The accumulations can be taken out in a lump sum (not usually a good idea as the amounts will be taxed at the highest marginal rate at that time) but most commonly will be transferred to an investment that will enable a periodic taxable income from this source: either annuities (which provides for equal monthly payments over a period of time) or a Registered Retirement Income Funds (RRIF), which provides for gradually increasing withdrawals over time. That's the theory. However, in fact, current RRIF holders who have securities may experience RRIF pension amounts that plummet in the future.

We all know of a grandma who hesitates to use any of the RRSP deposits her husband left to her, so concerned to pass this capital on to her children. However, we also know that on the death of a single taxpayer or last surviving spouse, remaining capital and earnings within Registered Retirement Savings Plans will be added in full to income on the final return, usually spiking the income to the top tax bracket, or into a bracket that requires taxation at a higher marginal rate than when the taxpayer was alive.

When it comes to taking income from an RRSP, you do want to be sure you "top up to bracket." Grandma understands the difference between paying at the top marginal rates (46% in some jurisdictions) and the lowest rates (25% or less depending on where you live). Taxpayers in low tax brackets want to be sure they withdraw funds up to the top of their current tax bracket. Your tax professional can help with this. Often taxpayers pay lower taxes when RRSP income is generated throughout a lifetime.

An orderly "melt-down" of the funds should therefore be planned. If the money is not needed, the tax-paid funds can be reinvested into a Tax-Free Savings Account and, after this, a non-registered account to continue to build and grow to use in gifting during life or at the time of death.

Practice Pension Income Splitting with RRSPs

It is sad when you see a couple who has made a mistake saving in their RRSPs. High income earners often invest in an RRSP only in their name, and later want to split half of the pension income from that source on their spouse's return. This is not possible until the pensioner reaches 65. Instead, contributions to a spousal RRSP should have been made along the way.

Here's what you need to know: taxpayers may contribute to their own RRSPs based on available RRSP contribution room, but may also contribute some or all of the amounts to a spousal RRSP. Deductions are allowed on the contributor's return, so that person still gets the immediate tax advantage. Age ineligible taxpayers may also continue to contribute, based on their own RRSP contribution room, to a spousal RRSP if their spouse is under 72 years old.

Also, it can make sense to practice income splitting with the RRSP, which is not subject to the Attribution Rules. By equalizing RRSP accumulations throughout a couple's lifetime, pension withdrawals later in life are equalized and the family unit as a whole can benefit from the use of both spouses' or partners' personal amounts and graduated tax rates. There is a restriction to be aware of: withdrawal from a spousal RRSP may be income of the annuitant or of the contributor, depending on when the last contribution to the spousal RRSP was made. To avoid this, wait three years from the date of that last contribution.

When it comes time to take the pension, annuity payments received out of an RRSP by those who are over the age of 64 (or those under 65 and receiving the amounts as a result of the spouse's death) are eligible for the pension income amount, and therefore pension income splitting on up to 50% of the income being reported.

Also remember that certain portions of retiring allowances may be transferred to an RRSP on a tax-free basis, for services rendered by an employee before 1996. Using unused RRSP contribution room when retiring allowances are received is smart not just from the point of view of avoiding tax, but also with an eye to pension income splitting opportunities.

Remember in planning your pension income that withdrawals from an RRSP will be subject to withholding tax at the following rates:

Up to $5,000	10%
$5,000 to $15,000	20%
Above $15,000	30%

The one exception to this rule is that amounts contributed to the taxpayer's RRSP and not yet deducted may be withdrawn tax-free and with no withholding taxes.

Back to School Thanks to the RRSP

While in the plan, the tax on income earned is deferred and grows on a tax-free basis. When funds are withdrawn, both principal and earnings are taxable. However, even retirees may use those funds on a tax-free basis for two specific purposes: to return to post-secondary school under the Lifelong Learning Plan (LLP) or buy a retirement home using the Home Buyers' Plan (HBP). Discuss these options with your tax advisor. However there is a red flag for the use of the LLP and HBP by seniors as the amounts must be paid back before age 72.

REAPING THE MOST FROM PUBLIC PENSIONS

There are two things to know about your public pensions:

- **Old Age Security:** This begins at age 65; you'll want to apply for it a couple of months before that. The big issue is to avoid the OAS Clawback, which happens when your net income on the tax return exceeds approximately $66,000. Those who are age 65 will also qualify for an Age Credit on the tax return. Speak to your tax advisor about avoiding clawbacks of this amount too, which begins when income is just over $32,000.

- **Canada Pension Plan:** There are several planning issues here, the main one being, do I take it early? Yes, generally that's to your advantage when you factor in that you'll have use of the money sooner, and you won't be paying premiums to the plan.

  In addition, benefits can be split with your spouse. That's good planning, too. You can start taking this pension at age 60, but to qualify you have to stop receiving actively earned income that exceeds the maximum CPP pension amount for two months. Once you've met that criteria, you can resume your employment or work activities as usual.

INVESTMENT INCOME PLANNING

With the exception of withdrawals from the Tax-Free Savings Account, tapping into income from non-registered investments requires tax reporting. So you'll want to avoid this and use other methods of funding your needs. The following summary provides a review of income and assets available for retirement income planning, together with comments on their tax-efficiency rating:

- **GIC/Bond interest:** not tax-efficient, 100% of accrued earnings are added to income. This means that even if you don't receive the money from a compounding investment, taxes must be paid on what is accrued.

- **Dividends from preferred and common shareholdings:** this income source can be extremely tax-efficient, depending on where you live and can even offset other income of the year. However, be careful; an overweighting in dividend income can cause a clawback of Old Age Security benefits. Benefits also differ if the shares are from public or private corporations.

- **Accrued value in income-producing assets:** Very tax-efficient, as those gains will not be taxed until disposition. Then only 50% of the gain is taxable.

- **Prescribed annuities and income trust income:** this income can be tax-efficient as it is made up of a combination of tax paid capital and earnings.

- **Mutual fund distributions:** Regular distributions from the fund: capital gains, interest and dividends have a variety of tax consequences. Generally you'll want to buy these investments at the beginning rather than the end of the year to avoid receiving all the distributions over a short ownership period. You will also want to inquire about corporate class funds for better tax-efficiency.

- **Mutual fund T-SWP structures:** A scheduled withdrawal may be arranged to some tax-efficiency.

MANAGING TAX INSTALMENTS

Note that taxpayers who must make quarterly instalment payments are those who owe CRA a balance of tax in the current year and either of the preceding two years in an amount of $3000 or more. Retirement income structure must always take this into account as overpayment instalments is common, particularly with new income splitting rules, and this should be avoided at all costs.

Principle Mastery: Stay focused on a long term vision for continued capital accumulation, preservation and growth, even in retirement. The byproducts of this focus will be continued funding of your lifestyle. But the win will be a tax-efficient transfer of wealth to your family or community.

IN SUMMARY

It is clear that tax-efficiency counts. In fact, in the absence of tax planning, retirement income planning will lose focus on the source—and dissipate the capital that could be generated from the pension income. By using tax-efficiency in tandem with pension withdrawal strategies, the conversation about the retirement phase of life can focus on an "Age of Legacy" instead of the "Age of Ruin." Tax-efficiency makes it possible to have a renewed vision for the preservation and growth of capital.

It is also clear that families who can split income in retirement will really move ahead in wealth creation as compared to families who can't. If you're in that group—singles come to mind—it becomes really important to focus on investing in savings accounts that produce a tax-preferred pension.

THINGS YOU NEED TO KNOW

- Retirement income planning is the process of integrating the investment portfolio, and the tax return with the retirement plan to fund lifestyle and preserve and transition assets.
- Retirement income planning begins with the identification of personal visions and values which lead to a strategic plan for lifestyle needs to be funded.
- Pension income splitting is possible for those who earn qualifying pension income, and it can be lucrative.
- Retirees have a larger "tax-free zone" both as a family unit but also individually.
- Income should be planned to minimize "clawback zones" that can reduce the Old Age Security, but also erode away refundable and non-refundable credits on the tax return, which will cost you more at tax time.
- It is important for people on fixed incomes to manage their tax remittances very carefully. Never overpay quarterly instalments.
- Investments should be structured to provide for income that is tax-efficient.

- All of the income sources in retirement should be appropriately timed and "layered" to get the best after-tax results.

QUESTIONS YOU NEED TO ASK

- What is my/our vision for retirement?
- Can I afford to retire on a fixed income?
- Will my investments deliver through volatile economic markets?
- Will taxes erode my income and my capital?
- How can tax planning increase our cash flow?

THINGS YOU NEED TO DO

- Start saving for your retirement with the first dollar you make. You'll maximize your time and money and become much richer than those who don't.
- Use the tax system to help. Put 18% of your earned income into an RRSP—religiously—up to the annual dollar maximums to get double-digit tax savings.
- Then, save as much as you can in a TFSA—**Tax-Free Savings Account**—throughout your lifetime. Let's face it, the name says it all!
- Don't report investment income if you can help it. You will be forced to generate taxable income from your pensions. When it comes to your investments: Defer. Defer. Defer.
- Plan to split pension income and investment income with your spouse. That means contributing to a Spousal RRSP and splitting superannuation and Canada Pension Plan benefits. In the case of investments, consider transferring capital between spouses with bona fide loans so that the lower earner reports more of the investment income in the family. Speak to your advisors about this.
- Plan to be tax-efficient in making financial decisions about retirement. Work with a team of professionals.

MASTER YOUR TAXES
A Tax-Efficient Retirement

From a financial planning point of view, studies have shown that retiring clients want to consolidate their assets, simplify their affairs and find peace of mind. There are several issues to consider to accomplish those goals.

TIPS

- Who is most happy in retirement? The simple answer is: those people whose life has meaning. Therefore, the most effective retirement plans are those focused on values, beliefs and goals.

- The most effective retirement plans begin early in life: a structure is possible for saving throughout your lifetime to guarantee resources in retirement, and that structure is greatly influenced by a tax effective approach.

- Be prepared: consider the three greatest threats to retirement in planning for it: lower than projected investment returns, higher than projected inflation and unforeseen expenses that erode cash flow, including medical expenses and taxes.

- Income sources should be planned in "tax-efficient buckets" given that eventually a taxable event is mandatory.

- Vigilantly reinvest cash that is not needed to fund wants and needs.

TRAPS

- Remember there are two retirements to plan for: men and women of independent wealth often with different visions and goals.

- Most people are forced into retirement because of forces beyond their control: loss of their own health and the care giving of a loved one being the major factors. Manage that risk with the right insurance products.

- Portfolio design without a focus on tax-efficiency is a mistake. The tax return is a pivotal component of the retirement planning process, because the focus of your portfolio must be on short term returns. Tax-efficiency can greatly enhance this task. Work with professionals who understand this.

CHAPTER 9

Master the Process: Tackling the Tax Return

This [preparing my tax return] is too difficult for a mathematician. It takes a philosopher. ALBERT EINSTEIN

> *Young mom Michelle and new father Jason were having dinner. "I interviewed a new babysitter for Rowan today," she said between spoonfuls of mashed carrots. "Funny, she mentioned that she wouldn't be giving me receipts to claim my child care costs on my return, as her husband preferred that she received cash—apparently it helps his claim for her on his return. Do you know what all that could mean?"*
>
> *Jason paused. "Tax evasion, I think. Sounds to me like the money is not being reported so hubby can claim more to reduce his taxes, at our expense!"*
>
> *"That's not fair, though," said Michelle.*
>
> *"You're right," said Jason. "It tells us something about this family. Perhaps we should find a sitter who has the right ethics and morals we need with the important role she'll play in helping us raise our child."*

THE ISSUES

Documentation matters, yet most people find it difficult. The young couple in this scenario needed it to justify their child care expense claims on their tax return; a provision that's often audited. Without those receipts, their claims would be disallowed. That's the bottom line when it comes to Mastering Your Taxes…no receipts, no deduction. Working is just that much more expensive when you pay more taxes than you should.

A lack of documentation also puts the supplier of the services, the babysitter in this case, at risk. Without proper records, the babysitter leaves it to the taxman to calculate her income and taxes. This is never a good thing. She is setting herself up for interest, penalties, and lots of grief. But she is also missing out on the opportunity to contribute to the Canada Pension Plan, a private pension through her RRSP, and some tax exempt savings opportunities with the new TFSA (Tax-Free Savings Account). This is expensive.

The alternative—mastering your tax return and its documentation requirements—sets you up for a powerful relationship with the taxman; one that works in your favor.

THE SOLUTIONS

The most difficult part of preparing tax returns every year has very little to do with math ability or intelligence. That's good news.

It's all about organization. It usually takes longer to sort documentation than it does to enter the data onto the tax return itself. This is the major challenge for all taxpayers and a major impediment to the astute financial decisions we want to make about accumulating and preserving wealth. You need to get past this barrier to achieve your goals.

It's true: the better you are at bringing order to your tax documentation, the wealthier you will be. You'll pay less to have a tax professional do your taxes, year over year, they'll do a more thorough and therefore better job at saving you money, and you'll benefit from being "ready"— with all the information to build wealth, after-tax.

You'll also be poised to prepare other financial documents better—your will, for example. You'll also help out your executors when they are filing your final tax return. And that's just being kind.

With the methodology you will learn in this chapter—a proven and professional system for tackling your return and sorting tax documents—you'll better meet compliance obligations with the CRA by filing an audit-proof tax return. Consider it a blueprint for success in making the tax preparation process work in your financial favor, both at tax time, and all year long, rather than against you.

Therefore, the benefits of making the commitment to master your tax documentation are enormous:

- You'll be organized when it's time to prepare your tax return, not stressed.
- You'll be able to ask better questions about your tax filing advantages and rights.
- Tax data will be harvested in a purposeful, professional manner, a critical foundation of tax documentation mastery.
- Properly sorted files will make data entry easier, and more importantly, faster.
- You'll be sure that you have fully exercised your legal right to arrange your family's affairs within the framework of the law so as to pay the least tax possible.
- Properly sorted files can help you look at your tax filing status over a period of years so you can "tax cost average"— take advantage of tax provisions that can be carried over from year to year to reduce your taxes over your lifetime.
- The ever-potential tax audit will be a breeze, giving you confidence and peace of mind.
- You'll make and save more money by taking advantage of fast filing methods, as well as the right tax theory options you have discussed with your tax advisors.

Best of all, mastery is simple, boiling down to three basic steps:

1. Understanding the components of the tax return itself
2. Setting up the files for safe keeping
3. Sorting receipts for tax preparation

To master the documentation requirements that thwart financial decision making for so many taxpayers, start with the end in mind: your tax return. This is could be one of the most significant financial documents you'll complete this year; one that can help you save and invest more money and create more wealth. At some point, you'll need to understand it better. Here is a quick sketch of its component parts and why they are important to you.

Tackling the T1 Return

Consider the following carefully: aside from identifying yourself as a tax-filer, there are four basic elements of the T1 (personal) tax return which every tax filer should be familiar with[1] in order to better manage your intended outcomes:

1. Total Income	Line 150 of the Tax Return
2. Net Income	Line 236 of the Tax Return
3. Taxable Income	Line 260 of the Tax Return
4. Taxes Payable	Line 435 of the Tax Return (federal and provincial in every province but Quebec: there a separate provincial return is filed)

Total Income, Line 150, takes into account the amounts "realized" or reportable for tax purposes in a year. This includes:

- Employment income
- The full amount of interest earnings received or accrued
- Taxable Dividends
- Taxable Capital Gains
- Net rental income
- Net self-employment income

---

[1] Go ahead, pull out a tax return and take a look at these line numbers!

Your goal is to find ways to pay less tax on your income, and defer paying taxes into the future, to better use your left over resources to build wealth. One way to do this is to plan to earn more of several types of income sources. That way you can "average down" the rate of tax you pay.

Net Income, Line 236, is what you are left with when you reduce your total income with deductions like the RRSP you contributed to or your child care expenses. Digging for every deduction you are entitled to is always important. Because we pay more tax the higher our income rises, every deduction used to reduce that income is proportionately more valuable.

Net Income is also the most important figure on the tax return, when it comes to the redistribution of wealth in Canada. It is used to determine the level of Old Age Security seniors will receive each month, how much Employment Insurance you get to keep when you've lost your job, and the size of refundable and non-refundable tax credits you and your family are entitled to, when your income falls below certain thresholds.

- An example of a refundable credit is the Child Tax Benefit and the GST Credit. To obtain these credits you simply need to file a tax return, even if there was no income or taxes owing in the year. They are called "refundable" as they result in a benefit payable to the tax filer by the government.
- A non-refundable credit on the other hand reduces taxes payable but any excess credit left above this is not refundable to the filer. An example is the amount you claim for your non-working spouse or child, or your medical expenses and charitable donations.

There's more: the figure you end up with on Line 236 (Net Income) can also affect how expensive it is to use provincial services like fees paid at a nursing home, or deductibles under Pharmacare Plans.

How you structure your income sources can have a big effect on both social benefits and user fees; all of which directly affect your monthly cash flow. A common way to reduce net income is with an RRSP (Registered Retirement Savings Plan) contribution, an investment we'll discuss in more detail later.

Taxable Income, Line 260, is the figure upon which provincial and federal taxes are calculated. You will reduce this figure by various credits on a variety of schedules, the most important of which is Schedule 1, which itemizes your personal tax credits. This form will also be of assistance in help you determine how much tax should be deducted from your income sources. *That's important as you want to start eliminating tax refunds and start using more of your gross earnings right away.* We discussed how to do that earlier in the book.

Taxes Payable, Line 435, is what it's all about—the scorecard. It's the amount of total taxes paid to the federal and provincial government. It is the big picture, every year.

You have already learned that this is the figure you use to determine your effective tax rate—how much actual tax you paid on Total Income, Line 150. (Divide line 435 by 150). Your goal is to reduce that rate by diversifying your income sources.

Now that you know more about the components of the tax return, it may be easier for you to compile the records and read notices you receive from the CRA.

SETTING UP THE FILES

For most people there are three files to keep to be tax-efficient—and compliant!

File 1. The Permanent Information File

Certain information must be carried forward and available from one year to the next to prepare current and future tax returns properly. This can include information about:

- Family contact information, birthdates, marital status
- Investment transactions—like your unused RRSP and Tax-Free Savings Account room

- Balances of provisions that are unused and can be applied to either prior or future years: capital losses from investments, business losses, moving expenses, charitable and medical expenditures for example
- Records regarding the purchase price of assets of a business
- Prior Notices of Assessments or Reassessments
- Copies of prior filed returns or significant schedules

You'll find a sample form at the end of this book to help you create this file and gather all the information you may be asked for by a tax professional. Keep this in a safe place and keep it updated. It is a permanent file that will be stored separately from your annual tax filing records, so that you can discuss your finances on an up-to-date basis with your advisors.

File 2. The Current Tax Copy File: Audit-Proofed

This file, labeled prominently with the current tax year and the tax-payer's name on the filing tab, is the file that houses your completed tax returns and significant back up documents. It is filed for safekeeping once the actual return is filed. This file should be identical to the copy filed with CRA (destroy all draft copies), but may contain additional notes, receipts, forms, and working papers that explain how you prepared the return, in case of audit.

Generally this file is what a professional will (or should) give back to you after you've paid your fees for services. Neatly stored, you won't have to worry about these files again, until the CRA asks for more information, and even then you'll have peace of mind. It's all there, it's in order, in fact, it's great!

When you open it, it should have the following information in it, top to bottom:

- A summary sheet of the tax filing results from your (or your tax professional's) software program
- The Tax Return Jacket: Page 1-4
- All T-slips, donation and other duplicate slips, separated (one copy is for CRA)

- Tax schedules in their numerical order
- Auxiliary tax forms and worksheets that explain calculations on the tax form and schedules
- Topical File Folders (Investments, Income, Expenses from Business, etc.) with all supporting notes and receipts appropriately ordered, added and clipped.

That's it…what you need to know about filing your tax documents on an audit-proof basis. Now, all you need to know is what to do to "populate" your Topical File Folders throughout the year, with actual receipts.

SORTING RECEIPTS

Take a deep breath. You can do this! We are talking about two simple steps, one taken during the year, one at tax time. Managing the documentation that goes with the annual tax filing routine can be simple, but you need to be committed to a consistent rule: you will deposit every piece of paper you receive in a "receptacle" or "holding file". Here's how to do this.

The Receptacle or Holding File

Most people don't have time to sort chits and receipts in detail all year long, but everyone must have a place and some broad order for documents as they come in. Get a receptacle—a filing cabinet, a box, a cart—the size of which is suitable for storing your documents and keep it in a place that's easy to reach every day and drop papers into. Gather these papers together into **Five Topical Folders** with the headings:

- Investments: statements from your financial institutions
- Receipts: those which you think are tax deductible
- Income: from all sources, including pay stubs and invoices
- Personal Expenditures: from medical expenses to mortgages
- Logs: copies of day calendars, auto logs, appointments, etc.

Be meticulous about putting everything in these five folders on a daily or weekly basis. Don't waiver from this commitment. *When in doubt, save it.*

The Tax Time Sort

Usually around Christmas time and throughout the first couple of months of the new year, T-slips and other tax documents begin to arrive through the mail. Slip them right into a file entitled **Current Tax Copy File**, described above. There is no need to open the envelopes until the tax preparation process begins. Just slip them into the file as they appear every day.

Schedule some time before April 1: a couple of sittings to get everything in order. Use the Tax Documentation Checklist, found at the end of this chapter to help you do this. Use this as a cover sheet for the documents that apply to you in the current tax year, attach the documents behind it, and list any questions you might have for your advisors.

At tax filing time, the **Current Tax Copy File** is taken to the tax practitioner, (or to the office or kitchen table if you are doing it yourself) together with the **Topical File Folders**.

Now the information will be resorted into a data entry order that follows the basic elements of a tax return, which you learned previously:

- Total Income leading to Line 150
- Deductions leading to Net Income Line 236
- Deductions leading to Taxable Income Line 260
- Schedule 1 *Federal Tax and Non-Refundable Tax Credits*
- Refund or Balance Owing

You are now ready to enter the data into this tax return to your best benefit. And you have mastered your tax documentation process. Congratulations.

Now you can focus on building real wealth and your personal net worth: what you have left to work with after all your liabilities, including your taxes.

IN SUMMARY

THINGS YOU NEED TO KNOW

- You need to keep orderly records to exercise your legal right to arrange your family's affairs within the framework of the law so as to pay the least tax possible.
- The benefits of mastering tax filing and documentation obligations are enormous.
- Properly sorted files can help "tax cost average"— carry over tax preferences from year to year to reduce your taxes over your lifetime.
- Filing an audit-proof tax return will give you confidence and peace of mind about your tax affairs.
- Understanding the key components or "skeleton" of your tax return is the first stop to eliminating tax refunds so you can start using more of your gross earnings right away.
- Having orderly records at hand can help you make better financial decisions.

QUESTIONS YOU NEED TO ASK

- What has changed in my life since last year?
- Are there any new tax laws or provisions I should be aware of?
- Do I have all the documents to account for those changes on my return?
- What is my total income?
- What is my net income?
- How will my net income affect the social benefits and tax credits I'm entitled to?
- What is the total tax I will have paid this year?
- What can I do to reduce my taxes next year?

THINGS YOU NEED TO DO

- Set up a permanent information file for pertinent information about family members and carry over provisions.
- Set up a tax copy file for your annual tax slips.
- Sort additional receipts into topical folders behind this throughout the year.

DECISIONS YOU NEED TO MAKE

- Do I want to pay less tax?
- Do I want to make more of my expenditures tax deductible?
- Am I prepared to gather and save all my receipts?
- Will I use use the information from my return to better plan my financial affairs?

If you answered yes to these questions, you have made the decision to master your tax return and its documentation challenges, using the process to your advantage in making better financial decisions regarding the taxes you pay.

Principle Mastery: The organized taxpayer meets all obligations, maximizes tax provisions to pay less tax, gets more from government benefits, and is poised to pay less tax in the future. Mastering the tax filing and documentation process is really worth your while.

MASTER YOUR TAXES
Master the Process:
Tackling the Tax Return

TIPS

- Always ask yourself when you spend money: is this expense tax deductible? Then keep the receipt, and be able to retrieve it when it counts at tax filing time.
- Can I arrange my affairs to make my expenses tax deductible?
- Proper documentation will help you file a more complete and accurate tax return, quickly, and audit proof. All you have to do is:
  - **Work in order.** When entering data, always move from line to schedule to auxiliary tax form. Then go back to the next line on the tax return and repeat the process.
  - **Do it right the first time.** Take your time, enter information from documents and slips very carefully, checking each number before moving on to the next.
  - **Double check all entries.**
  - **Keep a copy.** This means all documents including completed returns and schedules, and evidence of acceptance with CRA. These documents will be required in the case of an audit so be sure they are filed in a logical order.
  - **Make it retrievable.** Expect to be audited if you are claiming discretionary items like self-employment income and expenses, moving expenses or medical expenses.

TRAPS

- Disorganized people not only file returns incompletely, but they under-use their professional advisor's help. Avoid this.
- Don't drop a shoebox on your accountant's desk and run. You'll miss out on an important education about reducing the taxes you pay next year.
- Oh yes, don't leave it all to the last minute!

CHAPTER 10

Avoiding Trouble:
Your Relationship with CRA

There is no such thing as a good tax. WINSTON CHURCHILL

Talk about a run of bad luck! Jaime and Surrinder had married young, raised their three healthy children, suffered through job layoffs in each of their careers through various economic cycles, and struggled to keep their home and lifestyle through it all.

Jaime started her own business during that time, while coping with the demands of family life. Both Grampa and Grandma needed care; kids' were in activities and school; life was busy. In fact, everything was going reasonably well until Surrinder's car accident. He was left with a broken back. Jaime's business could not shoulder all the costs the family had; in particular their growing tax bills.

That was five years ago. Although Jaime and Surrinder avoided bankruptcy, they were in trouble with the tax department: there were outstanding tax returns, taxes owing for the ones they did file and the interest compounding on a daily basis. They simply did not know what to do.

THE ISSUES

Poor Jaime and Surrinder. How could things have gone so wrong for this family? As we have learned, successful tax systems rely on self-assessment. Individual taxpayers must file a return on time, and maintain records to support their calculations.

After this, they must also be willing to be audited—something most taxpayers absolutely dread. Not only is it difficult to pull everything together to file a return in the first place, it seems to be even harder to pull it all out again when the auditor calls. As we learned, *when it comes to your taxes, retrieval is everything!*

What happens if you just can't pay? Many people simply fail to file, hoping CRA won't notice. Unfortunately they will and when they do, delinquent tax filers can be subject to a series of late filing and gross negligence penalties—which together can add up to 67% of the taxes owing to your bill, before interest, and of course the taxes themselves. Worse, if there is wilful intent to defraud the government, criminal prosecution for tax evasion could result.

There is much you can do, however, to master your relationship with the tax department—in good times and in bad. You simply need to know how to avoid trouble.

Jaime and Surrinder, in fact, were delighted when their tax advisor told them about the *Taxpayer Relief Provisions*. These special rules, applied in their case, wiped out penalties and interest owing on their outstanding taxes because of their hardship. It helped that they had been "model taxpayers" before their bad luck struck.

THE SOLUTIONS

The confidence to go forward with legitimate tax planning comes from knowing your operating parameters. Most people honestly try to comply with the law. When tax disputes occur, an adjustment and appeals process is in place to sort things out. Most of these circumstances can be negotiated to a quick and successful conclusion with CRA by following those specific procedures.

It's when you slip the numerous tax envelopes requesting more information or your tax payment into the garbage or on top of the fridge, that things can go wrong for you. There are three basic rules for avoiding trouble with CRA:

1. **File your tax return on time**, every year, even if you owe money and you can't pay. You'll at least avoid a litany of penalties including late filing and gross negligence, described below. Be able to retrieve your files in case of a future tax audit.

2. **Understand your rights.** When you are right and the auditor is not, your appeal rights can come to the rescue.

3. **Look, learn, and save money.** Use the annual tax filing routine as a springboard for tax avoidance planning all year long. Remember, tax auditors are historians—they like to look back at your prior filing history and events to assess if you reported your affairs within the framework of the law. You, on the other hand, are making economic decisions about the future. Your ability to communicate the difference between the past and the future can help you gain the upper hand in your relationship with CRA.

FILE YOUR TAX RETURN ON TIME

The average tax refund in Canada amounts to over $1400 a year or about $120 a month. With that kind of money at stake, it is surprising how many taxpayers file their tax returns late, or are several years in arrears on their filing obligations. This is just not smart. Here's why:

- If CRA owes you a refund, you'll not earn any interest for the time they are holding onto your funds until 31 days after you file your return, 30 days after the filing due date or the day you overpaid your taxes, whichever is later.

- When you miss filing tax returns, you also miss out on creating RRSP or TFSA (Tax-Free Savings Account) contribution room. That cuts out two important tax savings vehicles available to you.

- If you are a tax filing delinquent, your appeal rights can be limited when you really need leniency from CRA—in case of hardship, for example.

- If you owe money to CRA, you'll incur expensive penalties and pay interest from the day the money is owed. There are penalties upfront on the balance unpaid and then additional penalties for each month unpaid. If you have been late filing penalties in any three preceding years the penalties will increase.

- Delinquent filers may not fare as well under appeals for leniency.

Step 1 in mastering your relationship with CRA is simple: file your tax return on time. Paying penalties and interest is expensive and completely within your control—so why do it? Know your tax filing deadlines and stick to them:

Tax Filing Deadlines
- Individuals: April 30.
- Unincorporated businesses: June 15.
- Deceased individuals: When the individual dies before October 1, the filing deadline is April 30 for individuals and June 15 for unincorporated businesses. When the individual dies after September 30, the filing deadline is 6 months following death.
- Corporations: Six months following the end of the taxation year.

Keep the Records, But for How Long?

Just because you have filed a tax return and CRA has in fact accepted your return and sent back a tax refund does not mean you are out of the woods yet. CRA can come back and ask you for documentation to justify your claims—things like tuition, moving, child care, medical or business expense receipts—at any time within a three year period. In fact, they can request information further back than that if fraud is suspected.

Just how long do you have to keep those records in the closet, basement or back shed? Here's what you need to know:

- Generally, you will need to keep those books and records for six years from the end of the related taxation year[1].

---

[1] Note: Corporations are required to maintain permanent corporate records for two years following dissolution.

- If you really must get those records out of your basement earlier, you may request permission in writing to destroy your records before the six-year period is up. Do so on Form T137 *Request for Destruction of Books and Records.* This is not such a good idea, however, as it may be a direct invitation for the dreaded tax audit—a verification of your filed return to your records prior to destruction.

What Records Should You Keep?

T-Slips, sales invoices, purchase invoices, cash register receipts, formal written contracts, credit card receipts, delivery slips, deposit slips, work orders, dockets, cheques, bank statements, tax returns, and general correspondence. This all must be available for inspection by tax auditors. You can destroy hard copy if you like, but only if you have scanned images of the documents available. If your records are a little scarce, know that you can be fined. So err on the side of caution and keep them all if you're not sure. Also, know that a person who destroys or otherwise disposes of records or books of account in order to evade the payment of tax will be subject to criminal prosecution and tax evasion penalties.

So, make sure that flood in the basement actually happened, okay?

Seriously, if the flood or fire was real, a tax auditor would ask you to reconstruct the records as best you can to estimate your income, deductions, and credits. This would involve contacting employers, suppliers, and institutions to recover your records.

Otherwise, CRA can either assess your return without this vital information, or worse, prepare a "Net Worth Assessment", in which they do the estimation of your income and deductions for you. This is a bad idea, as the onus of proof in that case is on you to prove CRA wrong, or pay what they are asking for.

That's certainly losing control over your tax affairs, and can be very time consuming and expensive.

UNDERSTAND YOUR RIGHTS

Probably the toughest thing about a relationship with the tax department is that you might feel things are a little stacked against you. After all, it's their playing field, their rules, and yes, they are calling the shots. But it's your money.

Taxpayers do have rights when it comes to their taxes. You cannot be "bullied" by CRA. You have the right to object and appeal arbitrary reassessments of your tax situation by the government.

In addition, you have the right to be treated fairly under the Income Tax Act. For this reason CRA has developed the "Taxpayer Relief Provisions".

Taxpayer Relief Provisions

The couple in our opening scenario benefited from the Taxpayer Relief Provisions when their tax advisor wrote a letter to CRA to outline their difficult circumstances and request the cancellation of penalties and interest. In fact, here is what you can request, under law, when a hardship strikes.

Cancelling of Penalties and Interest

You can ask the tax department to waive or cancel penalties and interest incurred under extraordinary circumstances beyond your control, like failure to file or pay due to a serious illness or death of a family member. In addition, you can ask for relief from penalties and interest if you suffered a hardship because of the actions of the tax department. For example:

- The tax department made errors in processing your return. This is always the first line of defense when there are taxes in dispute: did you make the error, or did the tax department err? Both are possible, and this must be sorted out.

- You were not being informed, within a reasonable time that an amount was owing because of processing delays on the part of the tax department. Reasonableness is a grey area, but will be assessed on an individual basis.

- You relied on government publications in filing your return, however there were errors in material, which led you to file returns or make payments based on the incorrect information.
- Incorrect information was provided to you by the department, and you relied on that information in filing your return.
- There were delays in providing information to you or in resolving an objection or an appeal, or in completing a tax audit.

Filing Extensions

You may file missed tax returns to request refunds owing and ask that deadlines be extended for certain elective provisions, such as pension income splitting. CRA will accept your late filed return and send you back any refund. You can request this for up to ten years.

> *For example: Zack missed filing his tax returns from 1998 to 2007. While it is too late to file his 1998 return (that had to be done by December 31, 2008) Zack can file returns from 1999 forward and claim his missed refunds. Interest on any tax overpayments, however, will only be paid by CRA from the later of the day after he overpaid his taxes, 31 days after the filing due date or the 31st day after he files his return.*

Adjustments for Errors and Omissions

You may ask CRA to authorize a reassessment of your taxes and credits and adjust your previously filed return for errors or omissions. If that results in a refund or a reduction in an amount payable, CRA will pay that to you. Voila—found money! And remember you can request these adjustments on an unlimited basis for the ten year period described above. However, again be warned that any time you open your return to scrutiny by the government a tax audit of other records or tax years can result.

Voluntary Compliance

So what happens when you haven't filed but you know you owe? The tax department will not charge gross negligence or tax evasion penalties if you file your returns voluntarily or report errors and omissions *before they ask you.* In other words, it pays to confess your sins before getting caught.

Understand Your Notice of Assessment

If your tax filing results did not turn out exactly as on your filed tax return, always discover why. This requires you to understand your Notice of Assessment. That's CRA's response to your tax filing: the form attached to your refund cheque or request for balance due. The Notice of Assessment is a very important document that should be kept in a safe place, preferably with your tax documents for the year. Here's what you need to know:

- **The date your return was assessed** by the tax department. This is important because that date is used in determining appeal deadlines. Check these out in the Appendices at the back of the book.

- **Your name and social insurance number**—be sure they are right. Your entitlements to things like the Canada Pension Plan, Old Age Security and other benefits are based on this information being right.

- **The tax year**—critical as you might get several notices, each for a different year, and you'll need to know the difference.

- **Your RRSP[2] Deduction Limit Statement.**

- **Starting in 2009, information about your TFSA[3] Room.**

- **The Explanation Section** on the Notice of Assessment details what changed on your return and provides you with balances of significant carry over provisions like unused tuition, textbook and education amounts or capital losses available to carry back or forward against capital gains.

---

[2] Registered Retirement Savings Plan
[3] Tax-Free Savings Account

- **The Summary:** significant figures from your return, as filed and as revised. Look for the figures that represent the basic elements of the tax return, and how they may have changed from the original return you filed:
  - Line 150 (Total Income)
  - Line 236 (Net Income)
  - Line 260 (Taxable Income)
  - Line 350 (Non-refundable tax credits from Schedule 1)
  - Line 435 (Total Taxes Payable)
  - Line 428 (Provincial Taxes Payable)

What's different? Did the tax department get it wrong or did you or your accountant make an error? If it is incomprehensive to you, get some professional help from a professional tax preparer. A pro can often help you determine the next course of action. It's important that you do that right away to preserve your tax appeal rights.

Do the following when you receive your Notice of Assessment or Reassessment from CRA:

- **Review.** When you receive your refund cheque or request for a balance owing after you file your tax return, review your Notice of Assessment as explained above.

- **Adjust.** If there is a problem, request an adjustment by filing a letter with the details or Form T1ADJ. Include documentation or an explanation to support your position. If the tax department refuses to make that adjustment you may decide to either pay the outstanding amount or appeal further.

- **Store.** When you ask for an adjustment to your return, or the tax department adjusts your return after issuing a Notice of Assessment, you'll receive a Notice of Reassessment. Keep both these documents, the Notice of Assessment and the Notice of Reassessment, in a safe place. They will help you identify investment contribution room (RRSP and TFSA accounts), business and investment loss balances you can still use to your advantage in future tax returns, and provide the deadlines you need to work with in filing appeals.

- **Object.** If you disagree with your Notice of Assessment or Reassessment after requesting an adjustment, file a formal Notice of Objection. This generally must be done within 90 days from the date of mailing of the Notice. However, some tax filers may object within one year of the due date of the related tax return. This is April 30 for most individual filers, June 15 for proprietorships, and March 31 for trusts.

  There are lots of reasons you should do this. First, filing a Notice of Objection will end collection activities already in progress. You may not be aware that CRA has the power to garnish your wages; that is, order your employer to send them the taxes you owe before you get any of your pay. That's important, obviously, as you'll need your cash flow to get out of your financial troubles. The Notice of Objection also preserves your appeal rights to court. A tax professional should be helping you with this process.

- **Negotiate.** You will be contacted by the Chief of Appeals to resolve the issue. Most taxes in dispute are resolved this way.

Filing an Appeal with the Tax Court

Sometimes, disputes can take a taxpayer into the court system. The Tax Court is the first stop:

- Disputes with the tax department can be heard in Tax Court if taxpayer relief provisions and negotiations with the appeals department fail.
- Your claim must be filed within very specific deadlines so be sure to get help from a tax lawyer.

Once you go to this stage, you should know that the tax department wins most of the time.

Collection of Taxes Owing

Just how long can the tax department harass you to pay your tax bill if you lose your appeals? It used to be forever, but recently the rules have changed. Generally, the tax man is limited to a period of 10 years from the date of assessment or reassessment to get blood from a stone.

But know that CRA is charged with the collection of taxes not just on behalf of the Department of Finance, which makes the rules, but also for numerous other government departments a taxpayer may owe money to. And it does have the right to extract your tax refund from pay, pensions, or future tax refunds to pay those bills on your behalf.

Use Your Taxpayer Rights

This is a final, but important point for you to know. *Unless you challenge the results* the Minister will assume its assessment or reassessment results are correct. In the absence of a pro-active defence, you are bound to live by what the tax department has determined the correct tax result to be, whether it is in your favour, or not.

LOOK, LEARN, AND SAVE MONEY WITH GOOD CRA RELATIONSHIPS

Tax-efficiency—the after-tax results of your personal and economic activities—can be effectively reviewed at tax time. When you take your filing obligations to the next step; that is, actually take the time to review the figures and what they represent, you will be able to learn more about what to do next to invest your time and money wisely to building a growing after-tax wealth.

Stay clear of paying penalties and interest on failure to comply with CRA. It's expensive and stressful and will thwart your good intentions to build wealth over your lifetime. Make it a priority to be a model taxpaying citizen so that if you have to rely on the Taxpayer Relief Provisions, you can.

Learn how to read your Notice of Assessment or Reassessment. Discuss it with your tax practitioner if you can't understand it. Use the information to get a better after-tax return for your efforts and save money, especially after a tax reassessment:

1. Rediscover your:
    a. Effective Tax Rate: the actual rate of tax you paid on your total income (Line 435 divided by Line 150 on the return or your Notice of Assessment).
    b. Marginal Tax Rate on various income sources: the amount of tax you'll pay on the next dollar of income earned.
    c. Eligibility for refundable and non-refundable tax credits, rebates and social benefits administered through the tax system. A complete list appears at www.knowledgebureau.com/masteryourtaxes.
    d. RRSP Contribution Room
    e. TFSA Contribution Room
    f. Your Unused Losses or other amounts which can be used in other tax years.

2. Learn about significant tax filing and planning milestones you'll want to meet throughout the year to stay onside and on top of your options for tax avoidance. A monthly schedule for some of these follows. Use this schedule as a guide for conversations with your tax and financial advisors.

3. **Stay clear of penalties. A brief list of some common ones follows:**

    Administrative Penalties

    • **Late filing penalties:** 1st time—5% of unpaid tax plus 1% per month for 12 months; second time within a three year period after demand to file: 10% plus 2% per month for 20 months.

    • **Gross negligence:** false statement or omission - 50% of tax on understated income; minimum $100.

    • **Failure to provide information on a required form:** $100 for each failure.

- **Failure to deduct or remit source deductions:** 1 – 3 days = 3% penalty; 4 - 5 days = 5% penalty; 6 - 7 days = 7% penalty; more than 7 days = 10% penalty.
- **Second time, same year, grossly negligent:** 20% of amount not withheld or remitted.

Criminal Penalties. In addition, for wilful tax evasion:

- **Failure to file a tax return:** not less than $1,000 and not more than $25,000 or both the fine and imprisonment for up to 12 months.
- **Tax evasion:** not less than 50% and not more than 200% of the tax that was sought to be evaded or a prison term not exceeding two years, or both, plus, on election by the Attorney General, an additional fine of not less than 100% and not more than 200% of the tax sought to be evaded or credits sought to be gained, plus prison of up to 5 years.

4. **Significant tax filing milestones** (Discuss these and any unfamiliar terms with your tax advisor.)

January

- Jan 2 – Reduce your tax withholdings at source: file your TD1 form to claim tax credits and a T1213 form
- Make your TFSA deposit
- Jan 16 – Defer stock option benefits
- Jan 30 – Interest payment on inter-spousal loans

February

- T4, T5 slips due
- Federal Budget review (dates vary)

March

- RRSP filing deadline
- Pension Adjustment Reversal deadlines
- March 15 instalment due
- T3 slips due
- March 29 RRIF recontributions

April

- T1 individual tax filing deadline

May

- Will and estate planning review

June

- T1 proprietorship filing deadline; June 15 instalment

July

- Portfolio review
- RRSP meltdown strategies
- Instalment payment review

August

- Child care, moving and back to school expense planning review

September

- September 15 instalment due

October

- Review family income splitting; interspousal loan planning

November

- CSB, CPB, investment portfolio review

December

- RESP, RDSP investments
- Tax loss selling, philanthropy
- Dec. 15/31 instalments

IN SUMMARY

Tax-efficiency can involve purposeful activity throughout the year, depending on your income sources and family size. However, it begins with avoiding trouble with the taxman by filing tax returns annually and on time, and refusing to pay penalties and interest because of your disorganization.

THINGS YOU NEED TO KNOW

- Your relationship with the Canada Revenue Agency will last a lifetime.
- It is potentially the most expensive partnership you'll be involved with.
- When you understand your rights and meet your obligations, this partnership it will be a smoother and less expensive one.
- Filing a tax return will help you reconcile, at the end of the year, the taxes that were withheld on income sources or sent to the government by instalment.
- Filing a tax return does more: it will also record your entitlements to the Canada Pension Plan, Old Age Security, refundable tax credits and investment opportunities under the RRSP and TFSA.
- Your Notice of Assessment and any Reassessments are important documents to keep in a safe place in case you need to adjust or appeal your tax filing results.
- Taxpayer Relief Provisions can be used to recover missed tax refunds due to errors or omissions or to request a waiver of penalties and interest when your filing delinquency is a result of hardship.

QUESTIONS YOU NEED TO ASK

- Why is my tax refund or balance due not exactly as I computed?
- What changed?
- Who is right—the taxpayer or the taxman?
- Should I appeal?
- What should I do if I haven't filed all my tax returns from prior years?
- Who can help if I can't pay my tax bill?
- What should I do if I can't retrieve my tax records for audit?
- How can I stop a wage garnishee?
- Under what circumstances can I request a cancellation of penalties and interest?

THINGS YOU NEED TO DO

- File a tax return, accurately and on time.
- File correctly: avoid penalties by correcting understated income or overstated deductions or credits on a voluntary basis; before they correct you, that is.
- Recover refunds: Adjust your tax return if you think you made a mistake or missed a provision that will result in a bigger tax refund to you.
- Ask for relief from interest or penalties: The Taxpayer Relief Provisions allow CRA the power to waive interest or penalties when you have suffered a hardship, the result of which has been your inability to pay.
- If you can't pay your tax bill: contact the collection department and arrange to pay over time with instalment payments.

DECISIONS YOU NEED TO MAKE

- Will I know where to find my prior tax records?
- Am I prepared to justify the figures on my tax return?
- Am I using the information from my return to make tax-wise investments?
- Will I be able to promptly respond to communications from CRA?
- Do I have a tax professional to go to if I need help with a tax audit?

If you answered yes to these questions, you'll stay out of trouble with CRA and enjoy peace of mind when that frightening letter arrive at your doorstep with a request from more information to satisfy a tax audit.

MASTER YOUR TAXES:
Avoiding Trouble

TIPS

- Always file a tax return on time.
- Be able and prepared to retrieve your receipts on a tax audit.
- Keep your books and records for a period of six years from the end of the year in which you received your Notice of Assessment or Reassessment.
- Keep your Notice of Assessment or Reassessment in a safe place.
- Use the "contribution room" figures on the Notice of Assessment to invest in your RRSP or TFSA.
- Proactively challenge assessments you think are incorrect; if you don't defend your rights you will lose them.
- If you owe, but can't pay, make arrangements with the collection department to pay over time. It will cost you interest, but it will keep your assets safe and avoid wage garnishees.
- File a Notice of Objection if you are in disagreement with your tax results. That will keep the taxman at bay and out of your pay while you sort it out.
- Make copies of everything that may be seized by CRA, including electronic backups.
- Work with a professional tax advisor if you have trouble...much easier on your emotions, and more likely to be successful.

TRAPS

- **Don't ignore correspondence from the taxman.**
- **Don't evade your taxes. It's expensive and it will result in a criminal record.**

Principle Mastery: There is no reason to fear your relationship with CRA if you are prepared to file a return on time and meet your obligations to pay taxes annually. However, there is no need to pay more tax than you owe in advance, and if you understand this, you'll plan your affairs to minimize your tax refunds so that you use more of your own money first, throughout the year.

CHAPTER 11

Checklists and Talking Points

There's only X amount of time. You can do whatever you want with that time. It's your time. LOU REED

KEEP UP WITH CHANGE

Fairness. Equity. Simplicity. Certainty. Neutrality. Compliance. These words described the ideals of the perfect tax system.

Every year, we try to get it right. We devote sections of newspapers and half days on television and radio deciphering the latest federal or provincial budget, the purpose of which it is to tell us how much of our income will be delivered up to the tax department to spend as they see fit, for the good of one and all. What do you need to know to keep up with tax change?

A. We Can Help

- **Buy** *Essential Tax Facts* by Evelyn Jacks every year! This book gives you the goods on the most recent tax changes and links to the indexed facts and figures you need to estimate your taxes.

- **Sign up for *Breaking Tax and Investment News* from The Knowledge Bureau.** It's free and it will keep you up to date with the latest information of significance to people trying to manage their "real" wealth—after tax, after inflation and after costs. Simply contact us at 1-866-953-4769 or www.knowledgebureau.com/masteryourtaxes

B. You Can Help

Choose a team of competent professionals lead by one trusted advisor who knows you well. (See *Master Your Money Management* for help with this task.)

Keep the documents to help you discuss your financial decisions with purpose so you can better accumulate, grow, preserve and transition real wealth for wants, needs and legacy.

- **Personal Net Worth:** Analyze and discuss your Personal Net Worth Statement periodically, but at least annually. Is it growing or shrinking? What decisions need to be made next to get the results you want?

- **Income sources and products:** Analyze and discuss your income sources. Are they tax-efficient? What is your marginal tax rate on each income source? For each member of the family?

- **Important tax and financial information:** Prepare your permanent tax files with information about you and your family that is carried with you from year to year for tax filing purposes, as well as to help you update your will.

- **Tax preparation documents:** Prepare your annual tax documents and file on time. A documentation checklist follows. Use that checklist as a guide to talking points you'd like to discuss with your advisor every year.

PERSONAL NET WORTH

A. Net Worth Statement.
As of this day _____ this month _____

ASSETS	DESCRIBE	$
Cash	Chequing, Savings	
Short Term Investments	T-Bills, Money Market, Other	
Cash Surrender Values	Life Insurance Policies	
Long Term Investments	Business Investment	
	Stocks, Bonds, Mutual Funds	
	Real Estate: Personal Residence, Vacation, Rental	
	RRSPs/RRIFs	
	DPSPs, Annuities, other investments	
	Employer's Pension Plan	
Other Personal Assets	Art, Antiques, Furnishing Vehicles, Boats, Other	
Total Assets		
LIABILITIES		
Short Term Obligations	Credit Cards, Income Taxes	
Short Term Personal Loans	Personal Loans, Home Mortgage, Car Loans, etc.	
Long Term Investment Loans	Deductible Mortgages, Investment Loans, etc.	
Total Liabilities		
Assets-Liabilities =	**Personal Net Worth as of (insert date)** _____	

B. Analysis of Net Worth

DESCRIPTION	AMOUNT	SUBTOTAL	PERCENT
LIQUIDITY			
Liquid Assets			
Short Term Obligations			
Excess (deficiency)			
INVESTMENTS			
Total Investments			
Total Long Term Investment Loans			
Total Equity in Assets			
PERSONAL ASSETS			
Total Personal Assets			
Total Long Term Personal Loans			
Equity in Personal Assets			

C. Analysis of Income Sources

How can you accumulate, grow, preserve and transition more wealth? It begins with tax-efficiency. Discuss your income sources and how tax-efficient they are in creating the cash flow you need to live and the capital you want to build for "wants":

TAX ADVISORY STRATEGIES	INCOME REPORTING STRATEGY	DETAILS OF INCOME SOURCE
No Taxable Income	◄── AVOID TAX	Avoid tax entirely with the following income sources: • TFSA Account earnings • Capital gains on the sale or transfer of a principal residence • Many insurance benefits including life insurance • The first $750,000 of capital gains from qualifying business • Capital gains on donation of certain qualifying shares to charity • Certain benefits of employment • Certain damage settlements • Damage settlements • The first $10,000 of certain death benefits

continued next page

TAX ADVISORY STRATEGIES	INCOME REPORTING STRATEGY	DETAILS OF INCOME SOURCE
Taxable Income	◄── TAX-PREFERRED	• Dividends from taxable Canadian companies; stock dividends, deemed dividends • Capital gains on disposition of common, preferred shares, mutual funds, exchange traded funds, options, warrants, certain replacement properties
	◄── FULLY TAXABLE	• Income from employment • Pensions: public and private benefits, foreign pensions • Employment Insurance benefits • Certain spousal support payments • Net income from Rental properties, proprietorships • Interest income: bonds, CSBs/CPBx, Annuities
Taxable in the Future	◄── CREATE TAX DEFERRED INCOME	• Capital saved in registered accounts: RRSP, RRIF, RESP, RDSP
Partially Taxable	◄── BLEND INCOME AND CAPITAL	• Annuities, multi-class funds, certain mutual funds, income trusts
Net Income	◄── REDUCE INCOME	• Claim carrying charges, deductions for RRSPs, Tax Shelters, certain personal costs like child care, moving, unreimbursed expenses of employment
Taxable Income	◄── SHIFT TAX	• Split income with family members: qualifying pensions, transfer capital with investment loans, maximize tax-free zones • Plan ACB levels: loss applications, residency, death of taxpayer • Use Alternatives: LSIFS, Trusts, Corporate Accounts
Taxes Payable/ Refundable	REINVEST TAX SAVINGS ◄──────	WITHDRAW SAVINGS ──────►

SAMPLE MARGINAL TAX RATES

At what rate will your next dollar of income earned by taxed? This depends on your tax bracket and the rate applied to different sources of income. Your MTR can be estimated as follows; amounts will change annually with indexing and federal/ provincial tax changes. The amounts below were in effect at the time of writing. For updating MTRs visit: www.knowledgebureau.com/masteryourtaxes.

PR	Tax Bracket	Ordinary Income	Capital Gains	Dividends From Small Biz Corporations	Eligible Dividends From Public Corporations
BC	Up to $9,600	0%	0%	0%	0%
	$9,601 to $16,946	15.00%	7.25%	2.08%	-5.75%
	$16,947 to $35,016	20.24%	10.12%	2.26%	-15.60%
	$35,017 to $37,885	22.98%	11.49%	5.68%	-11.63%
	$37,886 to $70,033	29.98%	14.99%	14.43%	-1.48%
	$70,034 to $75,769	32.50%	16.25%	17.58%	2.18%
	$75,770 to $80,406	36.50%	18.25%	22.58%	7.98%
	$80,407 to $97,636	38.29%	19.15%	24.82%	10.57%
	$97,637 to $123,184	40.70%	20.35%	27.83%	14.06%
	Over $123,184	43.70%	21.85%	31.58%	18.42%
AB	Up to $9,600	0%	0%	0%	0%
	$9,601 to $16,161	15.00%	7.50%	2.08%	-5.80%
	$16,162 to $37,885	25.00%	12.50%	7.71%	-4.35%
	$37,886 to $75,769	32.00%	16.00%	16.46%	5.80%
	$75,770 to $123,184	36.00%	18.00%	21.46%	11.60%
	Over $123,184	39.00%	19.50%	25.21%	15.95%
ON	Up to $9,600	0%	0%	0%	0%
	$9,601 to $12,003	15.00%	7.50%	2.08%	-5.75%
	$12,004 to $36,020	21.05%	10.53%	3.23%	-7.18%
	$36,021 to $37,885	24.15%	12.08%	7.11%	-2.68%
	$37,886 to $63,428	31.15%	15.58%	15.86%	7.47%
	$63,429 to $72,041	32.98%	16.49%	16.86%	8.09%
	$72,042 to $74,720	35.39%	17.70%	19.88%	11.59%
	$74,721 to $75,769	39.41%	19.70%	22.59%	13.76%
	$75,770 to $123,184	43.41%	21.70%	27.59%	19.56%
	Over $123,184	46.41%	23.20%	31.34%	23.91%

PERMANENT TAX FILES

The following information should be kept in a permanent file and updated periodically before your meetings with your professional financial advisors:

A. FAMILY IDENTIFICATION (For each family member):

Name _____ Birthdate _____

SIN _____ Phone (work) and (cell) _____

School _____ Address _____

B. CARRY FORWARD INFORMATION
Group A: Attach copy of previously filed forms or tax documents

- Copies of the Notices of Assessment or Reassessment from prior three years
- Copies of Schedule 1: unused non-refundable tax credits of prior years:
  - Tuition, Education and Textbook amounts carried forward (attach prior Schedule 11)
  - Unused student loan interest carried forward
  - Unused medical expenses carried forward
  - Unused charitable donations carried forward
- Unapplied minimum taxes paid in previous years (Form T691 Minimum Taxes)
- Schedule 3: Capital gains and losses reported in prior years
- Schedule 7: RRSP contribution room details; Home Buyers' Plan or Lifelong Learning Plan details
- Business and Rental Income Statements from prior years
- Capital Cost Allowance records: Asset acquisition, disposition and depreciation details
- GST remittances of prior years
- Undeducted Business Investment Losses of prior years
- T1-M: unused moving expenses of prior years
- Repayments of social benefits: OAS, Workers' Compensation, EI, government-funded plans
- Details of undeducted limited partnership, capital and non-capital losses of prior years
- Record of instalment tax payments
- Unused Labour-Sponsored Funds Tax Credits

Group B: Update from Notices of Assessment:

- Undeducted RRSP contributions and unused RRSP contribution room
- Unused Tax-Free Savings Account Room
- Undeducted past service contributions to a Registered Pension Plan (RPP)
- Capital losses or non-capital losses of prior years
- Undeducted business investment losses of prior years
- Capital gains elections made in 1994 – Copy of Form T664 from 1994 tax files

TAX TIME DOCUMENTATION CHECKLIST

INCOME SOURCES

Employment
- ☐ T4 slips
- ☐ commissions
- ☐ research grants
- ☐ directors' fees
- ☐ casual income earned

Public Pension Benefits
- ☐ OAS: See clawback calculations
- ☐ CPP: retirement; disability; death; survivor; child

Private Pension Benefits
- ☐ eligible pension and other annuity income
- ☐ RRSP or RRIF
- ☐ eligible pension income split between spouses

Foreign Pensions
- ☐ USA
- ☐ Other

Benefits
- ☐ employment insurance benefits
- ☐ universal child care benefits

Taxable Dividends
- ☐ T5 slips: grossed-up and a dividend tax credit
- ☐ T3 slips, Return of Capital amounts (box 42)
- ☐ self-reported amounts
- ☐ investment income from foreign sources

Interest Income
- ☐ T3 and T5 slips
- ☐ self-reported amounts, interest from inter-spousal loans
- ☐ investment income from foreign sources

Partnership Income or Losses
- ☐ statements / T5013 slips
- ☐ resource investment statements
- ☐ income from certified films and productions

Rental Income
- ☐ gross income
- ☐ expenses
- ☐ capital asset acquisitions and dispositions

Support Payments
- ☐ gross and taxable income
- ☐ agreement details
- ☐ RRSP-earned income may be affected

Capital Gains
- ☐ proceeds of disposition on capital assets (self-reported)
- ☐ T4PS, T3, T5, T5013 slips
- ☐ adjusted cost base and expense details
- ☐ mortgage foreclosures; conditional sales repossessions
- ☐ capital gains reserves (form T2017)
- ☐ capital gains elections (form T664) (February 22, 1994)
- ☐ capital loss detail (prior years dating back to 1972)
- ☐ new tax treaty rules help emigrants

Other Income
- ☐ lump sum pension benefits
- ☐ resource losses
- ☐ payments from DPSP
- ☐ recovery of exploration and development expenses
- ☐ taxable patronage payments
- ☐ taxable RESP or spousal RRSP withdrawals
- ☐ exempt scholarships
- ☐ RESP payments
- ☐ Apprenticeship Incentive grants
- ☐ workers' compensation, social assistance, supplements
- ☐ RDSP income

Self-Employment
- ☐ gross income
- ☐ expenses
- ☐ capital asset acquisitions; dispositions

DEDUCTIONS

- [ ] RPP: discuss new phased-in retirement rules
- [ ] RRSP—current and prior year contributions
- [ ] union or professional dues
- [ ] pension income split to spouse
- [ ] other employee expenses; Form T2200 (employer-signed)
- [ ] family: child care; child support; moving expenses
- [ ] disability supports expenses
- [ ] business investment losses
- [ ] carrying charges: interest; safety deposit box; investment counsel
- [ ] exploration and development costs; depletion allowances
- [ ] stock option and shares deduction
- [ ] other: refund of RRSP; other RRSP/RRIF deductions; repayment of RDSP or government benefits; legal expenses; CCA on Canadian feature films; foreign tax deductions; depletion allowances
- [ ] non-capital loss carry-overs: after 2005,carry forward is 20 years
- [ ] Allowable Business Investment Losses (ABILs), carry forward is 10 years
- [ ] capital gains deduction: $750,000 amount after March 19, 2007; $500,000 before this
- [ ] 15% of U.S. Social Security benefits, up to 50% of certain German pensions, foreign child support
- [ ] Northern residents allowances

TAX BRACKETS, RATES AND CREDITS

- [ ] federal tax brackets are increased through indexing
- [ ] basic personal amount and spousal amount
- [ ] Credit for each minor child, infirm adults
- [ ] Canada Employment Credit—no receipts required
- [ ] public transit passes—keep receipts
- [ ] disability credit for those with multiple medical restrictions, or those requiring extensive life- sustaining therapy, or those with certain memory impairments
- [ ] tuition/education/textbook amounts— T2202 required
- [ ] children's fitness credit requires receipts for sporting activities of those under 16; 18 if disabled
- [ ] medical expenses
- [ ] charitable donations include tax-free rollovers of publicly listed securities
- [ ] political contributions
- [ ] labour-sponsored investment funds
- [ ] quarterly tax instalments
- [ ] Provincial refundable tax credits: rent and property tax receipts

 **Knowledge Bureau**

Learn more with
KB 24/7 Self Study Courses

Certificate of Achievement in Personal Finance
- Tax-Efficient Retirement Income Planning
- Introduction to Computer-Based Personal Tax Preparation
- Basic Bookkeeping for Business
- Tax Planning for the Small Business Owner
- Death of a Taxpayer
- Use of Trusts in Tax and Estate Planning
- Financial Literacy: The Relationship Between Risk and Return
- Medical Perspective on Elder Care

KB LIVE:
Real Wealth Management Workshops
- January Tax and Wealth Advisory Tour
- June Distinguished Advisor Tour
- October Client Relationship Tour
- November Year End Planning Tour

Distinguished Advisor Conference

Financial Forum

KB ENEWS AND NOTES:
Evergreen Explanatory Notes: Your electronic gateway to tax information

KB Tools
- Family Business Succession Map
- Financial Literacy Tools
- Retirement Income Projectors
- Tax Estimators

KB Books
- Essential Tax Facts
- Master Your Taxes
- Master Your Retirement
- Master Your Relationship with Advisors
- Master Your Investments

FOR MORE INFORMATION VISIT:
www.knowledgebureau.com or call 1-866-953-4769

Index

Bibliography

Canadamortgage.com

Department of Finance: Budget Documents and Economic Statements: March 19, 2007, October 30, 2007, February 26, 2008, November 27, 2008; Tax Relief for Seniors.

Essential Tax Facts, 2009 Edition, Knowledge Bureau Inc.

EverGreen Explanatory Notes, 2008, Knowledge Bureau Inc.

HRDC: Canada's Aging Population.

Investopedia.com, a Forbes Company, 2007.

Knowledge Bureau Certificate Courses:
   Nelson & Jacks: Tax Efficient Retirement Income Planning.
   Nelson & Ironside: Portfolio Construction for Real Wealth Management; Financial Literacy—The Relationship Between Risk and Return.

Public Health Agency of Canada: Aging and Seniors.

Statistics Canada:

   Retirement Savings Through RPPs and RRSPs 1999.

   Pension Plans in Canada, 2000.

   Retirement Issues, 2001.

   Is Inflation Higher for Seniors, 2001 Survey of Household Spending and the CPI, Chiru.

   Survey of Financial Security, 2005.

   New Frontiers of Research on Retirement, Stone, Editor in Chief, 2006 Minister of Industry.

   Wealth of Canadians 2005, 2007.

   The Wealth of Canadians: An overview of the survey of financial security 2005 by Pensions and Wealth Surveys Section of Statistics Canada, released in September 2007.

Standard & Poor source for credit ratings, indices, investment research, risk evaluation and data, 2008.

The Case for Marriage: Why Married People Are Happier, Healthier, and Better Off Financially, Linda Waite and Maggie Gallagher, Doubleday, 2000.

Understanding the Time Value of Money, Shauna Carter.

Other Titles in
The Knowledge Bureau's
Master Your Series

Only from
The Knowledge Bureau

MASTER
Your Retirement

How to fulfill your dreams
with peace of mind

Douglas V. Nelson MFA, CFP, CLU

FINANCIAL EDUCATION FOR DECISION MAKERS

Only from
The Knowledge Bureau

MASTER
Your Money
Management

◆━━━━◆

How to manage the advisors
who work for you

◆━━━━◆

Jim Ruta BA, RHU

FINANCIAL EDUCATION FOR DECISION MAKERS